John Harley's evaluation of
to use a British expression,
examines their understanding of a covenant with Adam,
and in my opinion shows that the biblical arguments used
to defend this position do not stand up to the scrutiny of
Scripture. In this work John reveals his grasp of the details
of New Covenant Theology. I gladly recommend this work
to you.

Geoff Volker
Director of In-Depth Studies

A proper understanding of biblical accounts that transpired
in the Garden of Eden is essential to understanding many of
our Christian doctrines to including God, salvation, man,
sin, and so on. For far too long a systematic approach to
theology known as Covenant Theology has dictated the
landscape of Eden and imposed through "good and
necessary consequence" a deduced notion of a "Covenant
of Works" between God and Adam. It said that were man
successful in meeting the demands laid upon him the
promise of eternal life would belong to him and his
posterity. Additionally, in recent years a new position
called "Progressive Covenantalism" has risen to challenge
that view of a Covenant of Works, while still maintaining
the belief that there was indeed a sort of "Garden
Covenant" that forms the basis for understanding the
progressive nature of all the biblical covenants that
followed. But is there another way to understand what truly
happened, or did not happen, in the Garden? Yes, the view

held by New Covenant Theology which advocates for a solid biblical theology rather than a systematic theology as the foundation to our understanding of the Scriptures. By approaching the Garden account and the whole of the Bible in this manner it becomes clear that, while there was a relationship between God and Adam in the Eden, an oath sealed covenant was non-existent, nor even necessary until the time when sin had entered the world. I whole-heartedly believe that the work you now hold in your hands is most thorough presentation of the NCT view of the Garden and overwhelming response to Progressive Covenantalism and Covenant Theology's assertions. What many NCT writers have made attempts to express Dr. John Harley accomplishes to the fullest. Harley builds a well-researched case, exposes clear errors in his opponents' positions, and leaves no argument unanswered. While readable for the "man-in-the-pew," the academic level is more than sufficient to satisfy the minds of the scholar. It is with great enthusiasm that I commend this work to you for your consideration of the Garden and study into the Scriptures.

Chris Fales NCT Conference Organizer, Podcaster, NCT Porch Founder

A New Covenant Theology
Critique of the Adamic
Covenant: a Response to
Peter J. Gentry and
Stephen J. Wellum

A New Covenant Theology Critique of the Adamic Covenant: a Response to Peter J. Gentry and Stephen J. Wellum

Published by J. Angus Harley

ISBN: 9781717825308

Table of Contents

Acknowledgements

Gloria Deus! May God be pleased to bless his word. I am indebted to my loving wife, Tricia, for her support and constant encouragement to write. When I was down and out, she was the only one who got behind me.

Thank you to pastor Geoff Volker, a man who practices what he preaches. He opened himself up to contact, put me in touch with New Covenant Theology circles, and he read this book, making comments on it. What more can I say?

Thank you to Chris Fales for his enthusiasm in promoting NCT, reading this book, and encouraging me to publish.

I am grateful, too, to Stuart Bogden who gave me advice concerning publishing.

Abbreviations

GW- Gentry and Wellum

KTC- *Kingdom Through Covenant*

BT- Biblical Theology

NCT- New Covenant Theology

CT- Covenant Theology

AC- Adamic Covenant

NHC- Noahic Covenant

MC- Mosaic Covenant

NC- New Covenant

OT- Old Testament

NT- New Testament

INTRODUCTION

As the new kid on the block,[1] New Covenant Theology (NCT) has come under criticism for not having a developed theology of biblical covenants. Covenant Theology (CT) rejects NCT for it dispels various 'covenants' of Scripture: the Adamic Covenant (AC),[2] the Covenant of Redemption, and the Covenant of Grace.[3] Likewise, if the New Covenant (NC) and its fulfillment in Christ Jesus are a hermeneutical key to Scripture, and if the Old, Mosaic, Covenant is the 'villain', what do we do with the presence of grace in all of God's covenants in the Old Testament (OT) and especially in the Mosaic Covenant (MC)? Thomas Schreiner comments on Fred Zaspel and Tom Wells' book *New Covenant Theology: Description, Definition, and Defense*:[4]

> Surely Matt 5:17-20 is important in determining one's view of the law. Still, the authors provide little discussion of the

---

[1] I am not referring to New-Covenant *Theology* itself, which is found at various points in history, but to a self-identifying theological movement. [Cf., David H. J. Gay, *New Covenant Articles, vol.5* (Brachus: 2015), 118-138; Heather A. Kendall, *One Greater Than Moses: A History of New Covenant Theology* (Orange, CA: Quoir, 2016).]

[2] I distinguish between the Adamic Covenant, which was made before the Fall, and the Covenant of Grace, as CT labels it, the covenant made with Adam after the Fall.

[3] See Steve Lehrer, *New Covenant Theology: Questions Answered* (Steve Lehrer, 2006), 39-44; John Reisenger, *Abraham's Four Seed* (Frederick, Md: New Covenant Media, 1988), 129.

[4] Tom Wells and Fred Zaspel, *New Covenant Theology: Description, Definition, and Defense* (Frederick, Md.: New Covenant Media, 2002).

Mosaic Covenant in its OT context. They discuss the OT law frequently and particularly the Decalogue, and yet the covenantal context in which the OT law is placed receives little attention. They emphasize that the law cannot justify, but we are not given much help in understanding the role of the Mosaic Covenant as a whole. One of the key issues for NCT in the future is to explicate more fully in what sense the Mosaic Covenant is gracious and in what sense it leads to death and is to be distinguished from the covenant with Abraham.[5]

In response to Schreiner, we can say that, when compared to other systems of theology, the newness of NCT is a major reason for its lack of development in the field of Biblical Theology (BT), especially as it pertains to the OT. John G. Reisinger's little book *Abraham's Four Seeds* was perhaps the starting point for NCT BT.[6] There was the recent major work done by Peter J. Gentry and Stephen J. Wellum, *Kingdom Through Covenant: A Biblical-Theological Understanding of the Covenants* (KTC).[7] Gentry and Wellum (GW) were at one point self-professing NCT theologians but preferred the title

[5] Thomas R. Schreiner, "Review of 'New Covenant Theology: Description, Definition and Defense' by Tom Wells and Fred Zaspel," (July 15th, 2004), *R. C. Ryan Center for Biblical Studies*, https://www.uu.edu/centers/biblical/bookreviews/review.cfm?ID=72, accessed 5/19/2018.
[6] John Reisinger, *Abraham's Four Seeds* (Frederick, MD: New Covenant Media, 1998).
[7] Peter J. Gentry and Stephen J. Wellum, *Kingdom Through Covenant: A Biblical-Theological Understanding of the Covenants* (Wheaton, Ill.: Crossway, 2012).

"progressive covenantalism".[8] However, in recent days, GW have switched their allegiance to Progressive Covenantalism *per se* and opted out of NCT.[9] It is obvious why they prefer this title to 'NCT', and it is because Progressive Covenantalism attempts to trace out the elements of promise and grace found in the biblical covenants, which covenants, grace, and promise are fulfilled in the NC.[10] Beyond KTC, Stephen J. Wellum and Brent E. Parker more recently edited *Progressive Covenantalism: Charting a Course between Dispensational and Covenantal Theologies*.[11] And, once more, Stephen J. Wellum and Trent Hunter have traced the theme of Christ in the Scripture.[12] So, one could argue that a NCT-like theology is being worked out. But what about NCT itself? At this moment there is no NCT textbook for BT.

Another response to Schreiner is that, to this writer, his view seems reliant upon a presupposition of CT: he assumes that the presence of grace in the MC is something fundamental that is to be reckoned with. Schreiner's recent book *Covenant and God's Purpose for the World* shows a strong reliance on CT presuppositions. That is, he is heavily indebted to a covenants model of BT that stresses

---

[8] Ibid., 24-25.

[9] Thank you to Chris Fales putting me on to this. See Peter J. Gentry and Stephen J. Wellum, *Kingdom Through Covenant: A Biblical-Theological Understanding of the Covenants,* 2nd ed., (Wheaton, Ill: Crossway, 2018), 35.

[10] Zachary Maxcey, "Is There a Difference Between NCT and Progressive Covenantalism?" *Providence Theological Seminary Blog* (2016), http://nct-blog.ptstn.org/question/is-there-a-difference-between-nct-and-progressive-covenantalism/, accessed 5/21/2018.

[11] Stephen J. Wellum and Brent E. Parker, eds., *Progressive Covenantalism: Charting a Course between Dispensational and Covenantal Theologies* (Nashville, TN: B&H Academic, 2016).

[12] Trent Hunter and Stephen Wellum, *Christ from Beginning to End: How the Full Story of Scripture Reveals the Full Glory of Christ* (Grand Rapids, MI: Zondervan, 2018).

strong elements of continuity between the covenants.[13] Yet, in that book he does not deal with the stronger, grammatical-historical, evidence for the delinquency and failure of the MC. As important as the element of grace is in the MC, what about the overwhelming, grammatical-historical evidence for the failure of the MC and asking why it is that so many Reformed theologies put such a positive sheen on the MC? This surely synthesizes with the biblical, or canonical, evidence, as the NC's view of the MC is not only a hermeneutical commentary on the Old but it also fairly and accurately recounts the history of the *failure* of the MC.

My book could have been a reply to Schreiner's view of the covenant. However, I decided against this in favor of critiquing a similar position given in GW's KTC. It is a monumental work, worthy of the plaudits it has received. However, from a NCT perspective it is fundamentally flawed because its reading of the covenants is partly based on certain CT principles, not least of which is, the principle of the continuity of the covenants based on grace and God's covenant loyalty. In particular, I chose to critique GW because their model of Progressive Covenantalism was closest to NCT and because CT had already been heavily critiqued (and by no less than GW!). However, a full critique of GW's view of covenants would take a commensurate work to KTC. This book is more modest and takes aim at a facet of their thesis, namely, their belief in the AC. In critiquing their view of the AC, I will expose some of the CT principles that GW adhere to. I target the AC because, unlike in CT, the AC in GW's view of the covenants is the fundamental covenant, the one upon which the others are based. If one demonstrates that their view of the AC is wrong, then, in theory, one should be

---

[13] Thomas Schreiner, *Covenant and God's Purpose for the World*, Short Studies in Biblical Theology, ser. eds. Dane C. Ortlund, Miles V. Van Pelt, (Wheaton, Ill: Crossway, 2017).

able to 'pull on that thread' to reveal a line of theological weakness in their overall thesis.

I am not the first to evaluate GW, but my book is a more extended attempt at bringing to bear a critique. Of course, I am aware of the warm reception GW's book has received from a few in NCT circles.[14] I personally think that their work is so outstanding that it re-sets the BT bar for all of the players (CT, Dispensationalism, and NCT itself). It was only right that GW's book KTC, and its smaller brother, *God's Kingdom Through God's Covenant: A Concise Biblical Theology*,[15] were welcomed as a boon to BT. Yet, as one would expect, reviews were not always flattering. In particular, Dispensationalism is less enchanted. Jared Compton maintains that KTC " "fell like a bomb on the playground of the [biblical] theologians…" ".[16] [parenthesis his] Although appreciative of parts of KTC, Craig Blaising, Michael Grisanti, and Darrel Bock bring some significant criticism to bear, writing that the book offers a " "thin" reading", for KTC "is not fully informed by crucial textual details".[17] Grisanti dedicates a

---

[14] E.g., Fred G. Zaspel's review of *God's Kingdom Through God's Covenant: A Concise Biblical Theology* in *Books at a Glance* (August 26th, 2015), http://www.booksataglance.com/book-reviews/gods-kingdom-through-gods-covenants-a-concise-biblical-theology-by-peter-j-gentry-and-stephen-j-wellum/, accessed 5/24/2018.

[15] Peter J. Gentry and Stephen J. Wellum, *God's Kingdom Through God's Covenant: A Concise Biblical Theology* (Wheaton, Ill: Crossway, 2015).

[16] Jared Compton, "Kingdom Through Covenant: A (Dispensational) Review", *Detroit Baptist Theological Seminary* (Nov. 21st, 2012), http://www.dbts.edu/2012/11/21/kingdom-through-covenant-a-dispensational-review/, accessed 6/5/2018.

[17] Craig Blaising, "A Critique of Gentry and Wellum's Kingdom Through Covenants: A Hermeneutical-Theological Response," *MSJ* 26:1 (Spring 2015): 114. See Darrel Bock, "Kingdom Through Covenant: A Review by Darrel Bock," *The Gospel Coalition* (Sept. 11th, 2012), https://www.thegospelcoalition.org/reviews/kingdom-through-covenant-a-review-by-darrell-bock/, accessed 6/5/2018.

whole article to critiquing GW.[18] CT is also very critical of GW, as Michael Horton's review shows.[19] However, reviews from a CT background, although critical, tend to be more appreciative than Dispensational ones, a point I will come back to soon.

The reader should note that I am not writing from outside of NCT but from within it, accepting its presuppositions and general theology. From within this paradigm, I will demonstrate some rather large problems GW's theology has. I humbly submit that I am in no way surprised by this, as it is the most monumental of theological tasks to uphold a thesis on Biblical or Systematic Theology from the beginning to the end of a major academic work. I do not think anyone can do this with perfection. I will go one step farther to say that BT is the hardest discipline of all, for it is, compared to Systematic Theology, a relative youth.

My critique will specifically focus upon GW's defense of an AC and their positive evaluation of Adam as a covenant head and typological figure. I maintain there is no AC and that historical Adam is not a positive 'role model' for exegesis or theology. Rather, the Scripture focuses upon the promise of life in the Seed of the woman (Gen.3:15), the *protoevangelium* as it is called. In pursuing their Adamic covenantal-theology, GW utilize many of the tools of CT. So, interwoven with my greater aim of exposing GW's faulty conception of an AC and their incorrect assessment of historical Adam, I have included

---

[18] Michael Grisanti, "A Critique of Gentry and Wellum's *Kingdom Through Covenant*: An Old Testament Perspective," *MSJ* 26:1 (Spring 2015): 129-137.

[19] Michael Horton, "Kingdom Through Covenant: A Review by Michael Horton," *The Gospel Coalition* (Sept. 13th, 2012), https://www.thegospelcoalition.org/reviews/kingdom-through-covenant-a-review-by-michael-horton/, accessed 6/5/2018.

comments upon GW's overreliance upon many of the same principles that CT employs.

The breakdown of my critique is as follows:

My overall complaint is, GW rely too heavily upon the concept of an AC and a positive model of Adam, the first man. First of all, GW focus on a covenants system, which, like CT, puts pressure on them to tie all the biblical data into covenants. This leads to artificial interpretations of theology and biblical texts. At the core of this problem is the belief in an AC. Secondly, the AC is exegetically unsustainable as a biblical covenant. Thirdly, in explicating their concept of the covenants in the Old Testament, GW attribute too positive a role to the hermeneutical influence of the so-called AC and to Adam.

The first issue stated above, concerning a covenants system, is part of OT theology within a BT setting. The reason why it is important to look at GW's overreliance on covenants theology (not CT) is that it is the matrix out of which comes their theology of Adam and the AC. The second problem of the existence of an AC pertains to exegesis. The third matter of the assigning of a positive role to Adam and his administration is tied to hermeneutics. Yet, it is more accurate to say that each category and problem interacts with, and overlaps, the other. This does entail a certain amount of repetition of themes, although I think it is unavoidable. It is therefore merely for convenience sake that I will stick to these three aspects and their categorizations. My book will examine each subject in turn, always with the greater aim of undermining the concept of an AC and a positive assessment of historical

Adam. Finally, so as not to be criticized for merely criticizing and not offering an alternative model to GW's, I will end the book with a section that gives a sample of a different model of interpreting the 'Adamic' imagery of Genesis 1-2.

I will now embark upon my critique of GW by discussing their overreliance on covenants theology.

AN OVERRELIANCE ON COVENANTS THEOLOGY

What should NCT adherents think of the difference of opinion within NCT and Progressive Covenantalism over an AC? It should not lead to divisiveness, says Zachary Maxcey.[20] And GW assure us that they are not going down a CT route:

> The claim here is not that "covenant" is central to a biblical theology of the Old Testament, but rather that the covenants (plural) are at the heart of the metanarrative plot of Scripture.[21]

Is, then, the difference over an AC just a matter of opinion on a theological level? There is reason to believe GW do not think so. It is evident to all that they are invested in the covenants model. For that reason, I think they raise the ante, "one will not correctly discern the message of the Bible and hence God's self-disclosure which centers and culminates in our Lord Jesus Christ" unless one properly understands the nature of covenants.[22] One has to be careful with such 'never' statements. This is a similar argument to scholars who state that one will not understand the bible properly if one does not comprehend biblical languages.

---

[20] Maxcey, "Is There a Difference...?"
[21] Gentry and Wellum, *Kingdom Through Covenant*, 139.
[22] Ibid., 22.

Where does this leave the ordinary Christian, what about good translations of the bible, a disadvantaged teacher, or the Holy Spirit? At the foundation of the covenants, according to GW, is the AC (see ahead). It therefore follows that anyone rejecting an AC will never "correctly discern the message of the Bible and hence God's self-disclosure which centers and culminates in our Lord Jesus Christ"! I wonder how GW would feel at having this criticism returned to them and it being said that anyone who believes in an AC will never "correctly discern the message of the Bible and hence God's self-disclosure which centers and culminates in our Lord Jesus Christ"?

A Covenants-Dominated System

As an adherent to NCT, I am concerned that GW seem more concerned about a *covenant-dominated* theology than a theology that incorporates covenants. In their book, GW criticize various scholars for putting at the center of BT a model other than kingdom through covenant. In particular, we should note GW's criticism of Gregory K. Beale, professor of New Testament and BT at Westminster Theological Seminary, who places creation and new creation as the main themes of BT.[23] Yet, Beale adheres to CT. Kevin J. Vanhoozer identifies GW's weakness:

> Peter Gentry and Stephen Wellum also believe that the covenants constitute the framework of the biblical story, though they emphasize… "kingdom" through covenant. They criticize Beale for exaggerating the importance of creation and Goldsworthy, among others, for exaggerating the importance of kingdom. Their proposal has

---

[23] Ibid., 12-14.

the merit of seeking to integrate the themes of creation and kingdom, but without collapsing them into one another....They also seek to do justice to the theme of creation inasmuch as covenant concerns the relationship between the Creator and creation....

It is not necessary to decide which theme should have priority over others. While covenant provides a way to divide the story into several acts, kingdom keep the story unified.[24] [Italics mine]

Whilst Vanhoozer's summary is positive in its appraisal of GW, it does circle for us the heart of the problem: GW put covenant at the top, and not in some sort of general sense at the heart, of BT.

The same criticism is leveled by Paul R. Williamson. GW criticize Williamson for essentially ignoring Adam's pivotal role in the metanarrative of Scripture.[25] But why would Williamson incorporate Adam (and not only the so-called AC) when he does not believe in an AC, nor does he think that Adam had a pivotal and positive role in redemptive history? Leaving that issue for another part of the book, Williamson's response to the type of view put out there by GW is most suitable. In criticizing Walther Eichrodt's BT schema, Williamson writes:

> It is basically misguided, since any attempt to systematize the Old Testament by means of one central concept or formula will be overly reductionistic and will inevitably

---

[24] Kevin J. Vanhoozer, *Faith Speaking Understanding: Performing the Drama of Doctrine* (Louisville, KY: Westminster John Knox Press: 2014), 102.

[25] Gentry and Wellum, *Kingdom Through Covenant*, 164.

suppress parts of the testimony that do not
fit the overall scheme (e.g., it is difficult to
incorporate the wisdom literature into
Eichrodt's proposed theological centre).[26]

Not to put matters too bluntly, GW pass all BT data
through the sieve of the covenants and this leads to
mistakes.

'But isn't a covenant structure part and parcel of
NCT? Isn't this what "covenant" stands for in the name?' It
is one thing, reader, to teach that the NC must have priority
in interpreting Scripture, and quite another to say that the
resultant theological data must have an exclusively
covenantal architecture.

Even if one relies on a covenant framework, as GW
do, there is still no need to insist that the AC is vital and
that Adam is a crucial figure for *covenants* theology. No
less a theologian than John Murray spoke out against an
AC;[27] yet, he was a 'prince' of CT![28] Murray writes how

---

[26] Paul R. Williamson, *Sealed with an Oath: Covenant in God's
Unfolding Purpose*, NSBT 23, ser. ed. D. A. Carson, (Downers Grove,
Ill: Apollos, 2007), 32.

[27] John Murray, *Collected Writings of John Murray, Vol.2* (Carlisle,
PA: The Banner of Truth Trust, 1977), 47-59.

[28] The majority of CT scholars brush over Murray's disagreement with
a Covenant of Works, citing his agreements with its basic premises. It
is clear from Murray's writings as a whole that his view was a scathing
critique and no mere academic evaluation. What is often ignored is that
Murray lays out his own version of CT in his book *The Covenant of
Grace* and in it there is not a single reference to an Adamic Covenant,
Covenant of Works, or any discussion of continuity between the
Adamic Administration and the Covenant of Grace. [John Murray, *The
Covenant of Grace* (Phillipsburg, NJ: P&R Publishing, 1992).] Also,
his criticisms of CT were far from superficial: the term 'Covenant of
Works', he says, is not "felicitous", for the term itself pushes out grace;
and, there is no mention of a 'covenant' in Genesis 1-2, nor an oath.
The heavier criticism from Murray is the "grave misconception" and
"erroneous construction of the Mosaic covenant" that results from

earlier covenant theologians did not adhere to a covenant of works:

> Towards the end of the 16th century the administration dispensed to Adam in Eden, focused in the prohibition to eat of the tree of the knowledge of good and evil, had come to be interpreted as a covenant, frequently called the Covenant of Works, sometimes a covenant of life, or the Legal Covenant. It is, however, significant that the early covenant theologians did not construe this Adamic administration as a covenant, far less as a covenant of works. Reformed creeds of the 16th century such as the French Confession (1559), the Scottish Confession (1560), the Belgic Confession (1561), the Thirty-Nine Articles (1562), the Heidelberg Catechism (1563), and the Second Helvetic (1566) do not exhibit any such construction of the Edenic institution. After the pattern of the theological thought prevailing at the time of their preparation, the term 'covenant,' insofar as it pertained to God's relations with men, was interpreted as designating the

---

calling the so-called Adamic Covenant of Works the 'first' covenant; for it is the Mosaic Covenant that is, properly speaking, the first covenant (Jer.31:31-34: 2 Cor.3:14; Heb.8:7, 13). To Murray it is plain: the "Adamic", as he calls it, had no redemptive provision and could not be a 'covenant', therefore. [Murray, *Collected Writings 2*, 47-59.] Thus, today in OPC circles, John Murray is torn to shreds by some for starting a downward slide to the theology of Norman Shepherd. [*The Law is not of Faith: Essays on Works and Grace in the Mosaic Covenant*, eds. Bryan D. Estelle, *et. al.*, (Phillipsburg, NJ: P&R Publishing 2009), 15-17. In response to this, see Andrew M. Elam, *et. al.*, *Merit and Moses: A Critique of the Klinean Doctrine of Republicaton* (Eugene, OR: Wipf & Stock, 2014), 7-22.]

> relation constituted by redemptive provisions and as belonging, therefore, to the sphere of saving grace.[29]

Patently, to early CT, and to John Murray, a theology of covenants was not dependent upon an AC. Murray operated on the basis that a straightforward reading of Scripture put the kybosh on concepts such as the AC and the Covenant of Redemption.[30] That being so, CT obviously does not stand or fall with an Adamic *Covenant*; and there is no reason why GW's paradigm should be dependent upon an AC or the positive role of Adam.

A fear of a covenants-dominated theology, similar to CT, is intensified if we consider how GW's books (plural) read. Due to the dominance of the hermeneutical principle of continuity between the AC and other covenants, *at times* it is easy to construe GW's argument as identical to CT. Zaspel, a NCT proponent who praises GW's work, comments:

> Gentry & Wellum argue extensively for an initial "covenant of creation," the content of which appears to be indistinguishable from that more commonly designated as "covenant of works," "Adamic Covenant," "Edenic covenant," or "covenant of life." If in fact their covenant of creation differs in substance, it was not immediately evident.[31]

A reviewer with a CT background comments of GW's book, "There is no better defense of an Adamic Covenant

---

[29] John Murray, *Collected Writings of John Murray, Vol. 4* (Edinburgh, Scotland: Banner of Truth, 1982), 217-18.
[30] Murray, *Collected Writings 2*, 130-131.
[31] Zaspel, Review of "God's Kingdom Through God's Covenants: A Concise Biblical Theology".

than this volume. It is hard to imagine a better discussion of hermeneutics than can be found in Wellum's introductory section."[32] In addition, the reviewer notes that in CT the moniker 'Covenant of Grace' has become somewhat of a "convention used to talk about the unity of the covenants- a unity our authors recognize."[33] In other words, the reviewer recognizes a very similar, almost identical, model of interpretation used by GW when compared to CT. 'Similarity is one thing', I hear the reader say, 'but what about specifics?' Next, I provide examples of specific complaints against GW's overreliance upon covenants theology.

Example 1: Covenant Continuity and Grace: the Mosaic Covenant

In GW's account of the covenants, there is a straight line of continuity from Adam to Christ. This is similar in method to that used by CT, which draws a straight line of continuity from the Covenant of Redemption unto the NC. The golden thread running through all of GW's representation of covenants is God's covenant loyalty and grace. The gracious nature of the MC is reflected in the positive role of Israel within the covenant, a part that resounds with Adam's positive headship, "With this, we are back to the divine image in Genesis 1:26-28. Israel has inherited an Adamic role, giving the devoted service of a son and honored king in a covenant relationship."[34] The

---

[32] Joseph Minich, "Kingdom Through Covenant: A Biblical-Theological Understanding of Covenants," *The Calvinist International* (Nov.5th, 2012), https://calvinistinternational.com/2012/11/05/kingdom-through-covenant-a-biblical-theological-understanding-of-covenants/, accessed 5/21/2018.

[33] Ibid.

[34] Gentry and Wellum, *Concise Biblical Theology,* 144.

foundational role of Adam and his covenant for the MC is also seen in that the "Ten Words" (Ten Commandments) mirror God's ten words of God at creation, "he said" (x10) (Gen.1).[35]

Moreover, the MC is of a piece with the Abrahamic Covenant. The exodus from Egypt was in fulfillment of the Abrahamic Covenant (Exo.2:24; Deut.7:7-9; 9:5; Jer.11:2-4). The Abrahamic Covenant also shines the spotlight on Israel as another Adam:

> ...by means of the Israelite covenant, God intends for the nation to fulfill the Adamic role reassigned to Abraham. Through covenant, God will bring his blessing and establish his rule in the lives of his people and, through them, to the rest of the world.[36]

In speaking about the MC, GW refer to "the miracle of a covenant relationship of love, loyalty, and trust between parties".[37] Grace is the heartbeat of this MC, "the motivation for concluding and keeping a covenant with Yahweh is sovereign grace."[38] Due to the preeminence of grace in the MC, GW react to distortions of the MC:

> A lot of misunderstanding has been caused by contrasting the old covenant with the new in terms of "law" versus "grace." This text is clear: the old covenant is based upon grace, and grace motivates the keeping of the covenant, just as we find in the new covenant.[39]

---

[35] Ibid., 151.
[36] Ibid., 186.
[37] Ibid., 140.
[38] Ibid., 141.
[39] Ibid.

16

What, then, of the status of Israel's obedience to God in the MC? It, too, is positively assessed. GW focus their attention on Exodus 19:5-6:

> [5] "Now if you obey me fully and keep my covenant, then out of all nations you will be my treasured possession. Although the whole earth is mine, [6] you will be for me a kingdom of priests and a holy nation.' These are the words you are to speak to the Israelites."

The logic of verse 5 is that God has given to Israel a privileged covenant status out of his grace, and now the Israelites must fulfill God's expectations for them and become a kingdom of priests and a holy nation, a treasure for God, by obeying him.[40]

In truth, a proper evaluation of GW's rendition of the MC would take up by itself a full article. But, as their belief in the AC is my true focus, I will limit myself to a few comments. From what I can see, there is very little difference between GW's interpretation of the MC and that of CT. NCT must utilize grammatical-historical principles of exegesis. Yet, with this principle in mind, I am not aware of any NCT theologian who denies the presence of grace in the creation of the MC. It is not a question of grace as such, but GW's sanguine assessment of the nature of the MC as a whole.

Secondly, GW do not discuss the implications of the weaknesses of the MC *as a historical covenant*. These are not potential weaknesses but real, historical failures. The MC might have been created in 'grace' for the sake of Israel, have exhortations issuing from grace, be established

---

[40] Ibid., 142.

and confirmed in grace, but this is coming from God and says nothing about the spiritual condition of the people he was in covenant with. Still in grammatical-historical mode, we can say that the MC failed *as a covenant* on its very first day. This is a pretty big deal! Throughout the history of the *early* Jews, they are disobedient and unfaithful, so much so that, God does not allow the earlier generations to enter the Promised Land. Now, if the covenant fell apart on day one (and was, consequently, renewed, as GW described),[41] and if Israel was completely unreliable in its infancy (according to a grammatical-historical reading of the Pentateuch), we would be entirely remiss and negligent not to inquire as to the relevance and necessity of said covenant.

Intertextually speaking, is it, then, really such a big surprise that God calls for a new covenant? Israel got no better as a nation and was eventually cast into exile for its sins committed as a youth. Just as there is unrequited love, so there is unrequited grace within the covenant. Is this not why God divorces Israel?[42] Yahweh had had enough of Israel's whoring and unfaithfulness that it displayed from the first moment (see later in the book). But then again, Stephen has already laid the case out for us, has he not (Acts 7:27-43)? He does not resort to allegory, typology, the fulfillment formula, or any other hermeneutical strategy for reading the OT. His reading is a historical one based on grammatical-historical principles, surely. He recites a straightforward historical reading of the OT, following its 'organic' route, yet painting a completely different picture to that offered up by GW, namely, the Jews and the promised 'seed' according to the flesh were just plain nasty!

---

[41] Gentry and Wellum, *Kingdom Through Covenant*, 357-388.
[42] Ibid., 441-442.

Thirdly, the nexus between the grammatical-historical model and a canonical approach is the prophetic and promissory nature of the OT, yet GW do not explore its relevance for the value of the MC *in its historical setting*.[43] The promise of the Seed is given in Genesis 3:15, revealing that prophecy is present as a genre from almost the beginning. Prophetic (seminal Messianic) elements are surely present in the MC.[44] It is these elements that the Lord Jesus himself latches on to when severely chastising his own disciples for their ignorance of the Messianic message laid out in the OT (Luke 24:25; see John 5:45-47).[45] It is the same promissory and Messianic structure that Paul constructs his theology of the NC upon.[46] Yet, Paul sees fit to describe the MC in a highly negative fashion. In doing so, he is not merely critiquing the Jews for their sinfulness, nor the Law for its weakness due to the flesh, but he is rejecting the MC in itself. That is why *Moses* and his *glory* is contrasted to Jesus and the glory of the NC message (2 Cor.3). Even though the MC had a form

---

[43] This method is typical of many scholars today, some of which operate with history-of-religion presuppositions. [See, for example, Georg Strecker, *Theology of the New Testament*, transl. M. Eugene Boring, (Louisville, KY: Westminster John Knox Press), 34-37.]

[44] From a canonical perspective, I believe the whole of the OT is thoroughly Christocentric, not merely Christotelic as GW believe. [Gentry and Wellum, *Kingdom Through Covenants*, 120, 124, 617, 631, 714, 716.] However, in this sub-section I am interacting with GW's presupposition of the necessity of grammatical-historical exegesis.

[45] Their foolishness was not 'muddleheadedness' but rampant stupidity and unbelief in the face of the glaringly obvious (see Rom.1:14; Gal.3:1, 3; 1 Tim.6:9; Tit.3:3).

[46] Beasley-Murray captures the thought, "The Scriptures of both covenants bear testimony to Christ. *That is their glory*. It is also their limitation." [italics mine] [George R. Beasley-Murray, *John*, WBC 36, rev. ed., gen. eds., B. M. Metzger, *et. al.*, (Grand Rapids, MI: Zondervan, 2018), 81. See, Don Carson, *The Gospel According to John*, PNTC, (Leicester, England: Apollos, 1991), 264.]

of glory *because of Moses*, it had *no glory* in comparison to the surpassing glory of the ministry of the NC in Christ Jesus (2 Cor.3:11).[47] Likewise, even though the MC had a form of grace *because of Moses and the 'gift' of the Law*, it had no grace in comparison to the surpassing grace of the ministry of the NC in Christ Jesus (John 1:17).[48]

Another way of putting the same objection, from a canonical perspective, is that the presence of grace in the MC merely highlights Israel's temporary status as God's people within a framework of external blessing. The 'bread

---

[47] John MacArthur, *2 Corinthians*, The MacArthur New Testament Commentary, (Chicago, Ill.: Moody Publishers, 2003), 103-104; Ralph Martin, Carl N. Toney, *2 Corinthians*, Cornerstone Biblical Commentary, gen. ed. Philip. W. Comfort, (Carol Stream, Ill.: Tyndale House Publishers, Inc., 2009), 303; David E. Garland, *2 Corinthians: An Exegetical and Theological Exposition of Holy Scripture*, The New American Commentary, vol.29, (Nashville, TN: B&H Publishing Group, 1999), 177-178.

[48] David H. J. Gay, *Redemption History Through Covenants* (Brachus: 2016), 149-154; C. K. Barrett, *The Gospel According to St. John: An Introduction with Commentary and Notes on the Greek Text*, 2nd ed., (Philadelphia: The Westminster Press, 1978), 169. See Jeffrey D. Johnson, *The Kingdom of God: A Baptist Expression of Covenant and Biblical Theology* (Conway, AZ: Free Grace Press, 2016), xxii. We should read Hebrews 8:7-8 in a similar manner, which highlights the frailty of the MC itself. Some say that the fault of the MC is discovered in the people of Israel and that there was no actual fault with the covenant. It is said that God cannot create something evil; so, the MC in itself was not at fault; it was the people alone. [E.g., Philip Edgcumbe Hughes, *A Commentary on the Epistle to the Hebrews* (Grand Rapids, MI: Wm. B. Eerdmans Publ. Co., 1977), 296-297.] Yet, this reading denies the very terms of Hebrews 8:7 that say that the covenant was not faultless. The problem was the covenant, the MC in itself. What precisely was its problem? It was the occasion for discovering fault in Israel. It was unable, in other words, to create the terms it held out. That is why a new covenant was needed that could, by itself, create the terms which it held out. [See Thomas R. Schreiner, *Commentary on Hebrews* (Nashville, TN: Holman Reference, 2015), 249; David L. Allen, *Hebrews*, NAC 35, (Nashville, TN: B&H Publishing Group, 2010), 445-446.]

and butter' of NCT is that the MC was merely a picture of the NC in Christ Jesus. Any 'grace' given to Israel was superficial, a temporal blessing given to a physical nation, and not the actual grace of salvation, or even an overture of the grace of salvation. In other words, GW make the classical CT error of equating Israel and its covenant with the church and the NC.[49] I do know that GW maintain that the NT has interpretive primacy over the OT, and they reject equating Israel with the church.[50] Moreover, I know that they believe in a Messianic reading of the OT. *Yet, their grammatical-historical method ends up contradicting their canonical hermeneutic. This is to say that, they are operating with two interpretive systems that clash with one another and they are struggling to reconcile them.*

From this example of a line of continuity between Adam and the Mosaic Covenant, a line of continuity based on grace and covenant loyalty, we move to the example of the same line of continuity, this time from the AC to the Noahic Covenant (NHC)

Example 2: The Relationship between the AC and the NHC

Another concern is GW's application of the phrase *heqim berit* ("establish a covenant"). They maintain that the NHC is not a new covenant but the reaffirmation of the AC. God will "establish" his covenant (*heqim berit*) with Noah (Gen.6:18). This was not the initiation of a new covenant, because a covenant initiation is identified by the phrase "cut a covenant" (*karat berit*), and it is missing in the Noahic narrative, "the construction 'to cut a covenant'…refers to covenant initiation while the expression "to establish a covenant"…refers to a covenant

---

[49] See Lehrer, *Questions Answered*, 45-56.
[50] Gentry and Wellum, *Concise Biblical Theology*, 269-271.

partner fulfilling an obligation or upholding a promise in a covenant initiated previously".[51] At first glance it might seem that GW are saying merely that "to establish a covenant" entails that a *promise* of a previous covenant is brought forward into a new covenant. But this cannot be so, because an initiated covenant (a new covenant) requires the phrase *karat berit*. GW continue:

> Therefore, the construction *heqim berit* in Genesis 6 and 9 indicates that God is not initiating a covenant with Noah *but rather upholding for Noah and his descendants a commitment initiated previously. This language clearly indicates a covenant established earlier between God and creation or God and humans as creation.* When God says that he is confirming or upholding his covenant with Noah, he is saying that his commitment to his creation, the care of the creator to preserve, provide for, and rule over all that he has made, including the blessings and ordinances that he initiated through and with Adam and Eve and their family, are now to be with Noah and his descendants.[52] [italics mine]

In my assessment, GW want their cake and to eat it, too:

- "I will establish my covenant" = the establishment of *one* covenant.
- In GW's system, the one covenant that is established is the AC, as if to say, "I will

---

[51] Gentry and Wellum, *Kingdom Through Covenants*, 155-156.
[52] Ibid. 156.

establish my covenant that I made *with Adam*".

- Thus, the covenant *of Adam* is established with Noah and his family and creation.
- It is not therefore a *NHC* in any sense. Rather, it is purely an *Adamic* Covenant, and Noah and his family *share* in that covenant.
- The AC is renewed, but it is not redefined to become an actual *NHC*.

The reader might think that this critique is sour grapes, for, as GW note, Abraham, Isaac, and Jacob- three different individuals- participated in the one covenant, "God heard their groaning and he remembered his covenant with Abraham, with Isaac and with Jacob" (Exo.2:24).[53] GW read back this pattern of many-in-one into a supposed relationship between the AC and the NHC, and conclude that, to all intents and purposes, Noah was a leading member within the creation covenant.

However, we are again confronted with obstacles. The x-factor in the Abrahamic Covenant is that the three men (Abraham, Isaac, and Jacob) were leading members of the one covenant, with Abraham as the true head; the one covenant with Abraham anticipated within itself other leaders of the covenant that were incorporated in him, namely, Isaac and Jacob. In this setting, the term 'covenant' is always singular, state GW, and indicates one covenant made incorporating three persons.[54] No such reference is present in Genesis to describe Noah's participation in a covenant with *Adam*, yet this is what we would expect (see Lev.26:42; Deut.4:31).

---

[53] See Gentry and Wellum, *Kingdom Through Covenants*, 304.
[54] Gentry and Wellum, *Kingdom Through Covenants*, 158.

Example 3: A Form of Covenants-Flattening

I also believe that GW express a form of covenants-flattening. This might seem highly unlikely to the reader given GW's NCT credentials and because they accuse CT of flattening the covenants.[55] Yet, anxious to advance the continuity of the covenants, GW promote the belief that the AC is the foundational covenant and the rest of the OT covenants follow through on, and expand, this one, Adamic, covenant:

> ...the main point is this: the "covenant with creation" and Adam's representative role in the covenant is foundational to *all* the biblical covenants. In other words, whether we think of later covenants with Noah, Abraham, Israel, or David, all of these subsequent relations are a subset of Adam and this covenant. This is why later covenant mediators pick up the role of Adam and function as "little Adams," and this is why the new covenant, mediated by the "last Adam," our Lord Jesus Christ, is that which recovers the original situation, though of course in a greater or *a fortiori* manner.[56] [italics theirs]

Adam and his so-called covenant is given such a pivotal role for OT covenants that if one presses GW's logic one might end up with a form of the flattening out of the OT covenants. Each OT covenant carries forward the previous covenants, going back to the AC,[57] "...Adam and the 'other

---

[55] Ibid., 114, 125, 695, 697.
[56] Ibid., 617; see, 616, 621.
[57] Ibid., 383, 387-389.

Adams' who follow him are all associated with the covenants of creation, Noah, Abraham, Israel, and David."[58] This implies that Adam is a pivotal figure for future covenants. How so? In this way, "all of these later covenant mediators function as a subset of Adam"; [59] "In all of these heads, the role of Adam is continued in the world".[60] That is, the other OT covenants explicate the AC:

> Furthermore, Adam as a covenant head is typological of the "last Adam" to come, and as we move across the covenants, Adam and the land is developed in terms of Noah, Abraham, and his seed, the nation of Israel and her land, and ultimately in the Davidic King who will rule the entire creation."[61]

Consequently, the Abrahamic Covenant is also an expression of the AC,[62] as too is the Mosaic Covenant,[63] and the Davidic Covenant. Of course, I acknowledge that GW reject a Covenant of Redemption, a Covenant of Grace, and a Covenant of "Works";[64] nevertheless, the pivotal role of the AC and its centrality to subsequent covenants gives the impression that GW verge on a form of covenants-flattening.

Although I have now finished the BT response to GW, it will be objected that I have not actually answered GW's claim that *heqim berith* refers to the establishing of a previously made covenant. I have deliberately delayed an

---

[58] Ibid., 107.
[59] Ibid., 258.
[60] Ibid., 107.
[61] Ibid., 124.
[62] Ibid., 106, 226, 228, 247, 293, 303, 631.
[63] Ibid., 383.
[64] Ibid., 59-80.

exegetical response until the next section on exegesis, in which I critique the very existence of an AC.

2.

A LACK OF EXEGETICAL EVIDENCE FOR AN AC

The exegetical section begins with a response to GW's understanding of *heqim berith*.

Does Noah's Covenant "Establish" Adam's 'Covenant'?

Is GW's use of *heqim berit* and *karat berit* as airtight as they claim? Patently, to use GW's broader covenant framework, it does not require *karat berit* to be present for there to be a new covenant in a text, for the so-called AC has no cutting of the covenant ritualism and terminology. If the AC did not need the phrase "cut a covenant," yet a covenant was made, did the NHC need the phrase "cut a covenant" to legitimize its new covenant status? The absence of "cut a covenant" might be due to an innocent reason, for example, maybe the terminology was not used during Noah's time. (I do go on to propose my own reason for its absence.)

In the case of Deuteronomy 29:1, GW noted that the covenant that was *cut* was the Mosaic Covenant at Horeb and the 'other' covenant was, as GW say, supplemental.[65] The Deuteronomic 'Covenant' ends up being, "a renewal of the covenant with [Israel] as well as a covenant made for the first time as a supplement to the covenant at Sinai."[66]

---

[65] Ibid., 378.
[66] Ibid., 381.

- "Cut a covenant" invariably denotes a brand-new covenant; "establish a covenant" invariably refers to the renewal of a previous covenant.
- *Karat berit* in Deuteronomy 29:1 denotes a brand-new covenant.
- However, the brand-new covenant is *also* the renewal of a previous covenant.
- One might call this new-covenant a supplemental covenant, therefore.

Douglas Moo points out the inconsistency here: how can one covenant be, at the same time, both a new covenant *and* the establishing of a previous covenant given GW's strict insistence on the difference between *heqim berit* and *karat berit*?[67] GW's response reasserts their position, specifying the need to cut a covenant because the previous generation of fathers had broken the Mosaic Covenant.[68] Perhaps this is a satisfactory explanation of the text, yet, if it is, it means that GW have created a unique species as far as their own definitions are concerned: a covenant that is *both* a new covenant *and* a renewed covenant. In extending GW's own interpretation of Deuteronomy 29:1, one could argue that covenants have the ability to be at one and the same time both specific or new *and* a renewal. For example, the covenant with Isaac might be, conceptually speaking, a new covenant, for it might be considered

---

[67] Douglas Moo, "Kingdom Through Covenant: A Review by Douglas Moo," *The Gospel Coalition* (Sept.12th, 2012), https://www.thegospelcoalition.org/reviews/kingdom-through-covenant-a-review-by-douglas-moo/, accessed 5/28/2018.

[68] Peter Gentry and Stephen Wellum, " 'Kingdom Through Covenant' Authors Respond to Bock, Moo, Horton," *The Gospel Coalition* (Sept. 20th, 2012), https://www.thegospelcoalition.org/article/gentry-and-wellum-respond-to-kingdom-through-covenant-reviews/, accessed 5/28/2018.

'supplemental' to the Abrahamic Covenant; yet, one might also say that the covenant with Isaac were a renewal of the covenant with Abraham. In this way, one could argue that the NHC is a brand-new covenant, yet, at the same time, the establishing of the AC. And then, by extension, one could perhaps argue (if one were so inclined) that the NC were both new and a renewal of the MC. (Once again, I do not accept these possibilities are realities, but I mention them to draw attention to paths GW's definitions might go down.)

Moo exposes an inconsistency in GW's distinction between *heqim berit* and *karat berit*, for they say that Ezekiel 16:60, 62 breaks the expectations for the meaning of *heqim berit* and *karat berit*, for it is the *new* covenant that is *established*.[69] GW accept that this instance is a "hole in their argument", but they swiftly fill in the hole with the following change: v59 refers to the Mosaic Covenant, and v60 to the Abrahamic Covenant.[70] I think on this point of interpretation GW are correct.

Having said these things, I am not *in theory* against a *general* distinction between *heqim berit* and *karat berit*; however, the solution for interpreting the NHC is not to appeal to God's relationship with Adam. It just happens to be that the NHC is issued in the context of sacrifice:

> Then Noah built an altar to the LORD, and took of every clean animal and of every clean bird and offered burnt offerings on the altar. [21] The LORD smelled the soothing aroma; and the LORD said to Himself, "I will never again curse the ground on account of man, for the intent of man's heart is evil from his youth; and I will never

---

[69] Moo, "Review".

[70] Gentry and Wellum, *Concise Biblical Theology*, 217-225.

again destroy every living thing, as I have
done (Gen.8:20-21).

GW interpret these verses as referring to an appeasing
sacrifice.[71] Although, GW do manage to connect the
reference to an altar to Adam and conclude that Noah was
"fulfilling an Adamic role: he offers sacrifice as a priest
and worships God in this mountain sanctuary."[72] This is yet
another instance of eisegesis on GW's part. At the very
least, Noah's sacrifices indicate that God was appeased;
however, God has already cut off (*karat*) mankind by water
(Gen.9:11), and now the sacrifices of animals and birds
intimate substitution and that God will therefore never
again cut off man.[73] It implies that something, or someone,
will be slain in the place of man. Williamson writes that the
formal ratification of the covenant begins in Genesis 8:20
with the sacrifices. He notes a potential chiastic pattern in
verses 20-21 indicating that the sacrifices specifically are
covenantal in nature. Also, it is probable that God
anticipated these sacrifices (see Gen.7:2-3). Sacrificial
ritual is mentioned elsewhere in the context of confirming a
covenant (see Gen.15:9ff.; 24:5-6).[74]

When all is said and done, the Adamic
administration and the NHC are two different entities. The
former concerns the original creation and a time of peace
between God and man. The latter reflects upon the
necessity of wiping man out because of his sin and the need
of a covenant to prevent that from happening again through
water. Adam and his time are never explicitly mentioned in
the Noahic setting. Paul R. Williamson concisely concludes
concerning the NHC, "as a straightforward reading

---

[71] Ibid., 65.

[72] Ibid., 100.

[73] Cf., O. Palmer Robertson, *The Christ of the Covenants* (Phillipsburg,
NJ: Presbyterian and Reformed Publishing Company, 1980), 11.

[74] Williamson, *Sealed with an Oath*, 61-62.

suggests, here the concept of a divine-human covenant is being introduced for the first time."[75]

Nor are the allusions to Genesis 1-2 in Genesis 9 indicative of the reassertion of the original relationship between God and Adam. What these allusions indicate is that in spite of mankind's failure in Adam, which disaster is then re-enacted globally in mankind's rebellion (Gen.6), God is willing to destroy sin and its curse and bring mankind again into a living, sinless, relationship with him. But I will have to leave any further comments on this matter to later in the book when I unfold my method of interpreting God's relationship to Adam.

To finish this subsection, it is most revealing that GW's discussion of the AC comes after their explanation of the NHC.[76] In sum, their general position is a case of circular reasoning where one 'silent' covenant is used to legitimize the other.

The next sub-section is an extension of the previous one, as it discusses whether certain OT passages indicate a NHC that is based upon an AC.

Isaiah 24:3-5 and Jeremiah 33:19-26: The AC?

Isaiah 24:3-5 and Jeremiah 33:19-26 are set aside, by GW, as texts that refer to a covenant with Noah that most likely extend from it to the covenant with Adam.[77]

Let us look at Isaiah 24:1-6:

> Behold, the LORD lays the earth waste, devastates it, distorts its surface and scatters its inhabitants. [2] And the people will be like the priest, the servant like his master, the maid like her mistress, the buyer like the

---

[75] Ibid., 73.

[76] Gentry and Wellum, *Kingdom Through Covenant*, 147, 177.

[77] Ibid., 173-174.

seller, the lender like the borrower,
the creditor like the debtor. [3] The earth will
be completely laid waste and completely
despoiled, for the LORD has spoken this
word. [4] The earth mourns and withers, the
world fades and withers, the exalted of the
people of the earth fade away. [5] The earth is
also polluted by its inhabitants, for they
transgressed laws, violated statutes, broke
the everlasting covenant. [6] Therefore, a curse
devours the earth, and those who live in it
are held guilty. Therefore, the inhabitants of
the earth are burned, and few men are left.

GW read this and say that the "most probable referent", in terms of a covenant, is the NHC. I agree. The context of Isaiah 24 is that God is punishing the earth, the great nations of the earth, for their wanton violence and destruction. They had broken God's "law" given in Genesis 9:6-7 that forbade man from killing man, and they had broken the law saying man must be fruitful. In particular, many of the great nations had attacked the people of God and were now going to pay for it (Isa.24:21-23).[78] There is no need to posit an AC to interpret Isaiah 24:3-5, therefore.

Jeremiah 33:19-26 says:

The word of the LORD came to
Jeremiah: [20] "This is what the LORD says: 'If
you can break my covenant with the day and

---

[78] Otto Kaiser, *Isaiah 13-39: A Commentary* (Philadelphia: The Westminster Press, 1974), 183; J. Alec Motyer, *Isaiah*, TOTC, (Downers Grove, Ill: InterVarsity Press, 1999), 185; Brevard S. Childs, *Isaiah* (Louisville, KY: Westminster John Knox Press, 2001), 179. See Williamson, *Sealed with an Oath*, 65; Gary V. Smith, *Isaiah 1-39*, NAC vol.15A, (Nashville, TN: B&H Publishing Group, 2007), 416-417.

my covenant with the night, so that day and night no longer come at their appointed time, [21] then my covenant with David my servant—and my covenant with the Levites who are priests ministering before me—can be broken and David will no longer have a descendant to reign on his throne. [22] I will make the descendants of David my servant and the Levites who minister before me as countless as the stars in the sky and as measureless as the sand on the seashore.'" [23] The word of the LORD came to Jeremiah: [24] "Have you not noticed that these people are saying, 'The LORD has rejected the two kingdoms he chose'? So they despise my people and no longer regard them as a nation. [25] This is what the LORD says: 'If I have not made my covenant with day and night and established the laws of heaven and earth, [26] then I will reject the descendants of Jacob and David my servant and will not choose one of his sons to rule over the descendants of Abraham, Isaac and Jacob. For I will restore their fortunes and have compassion on them.'"

Verse 20 resonates with Noahic language:

> "While the earth remains,
> Seedtime and harvest,
> And cold and heat,
> And summer and winter,
> And day and night
> Shall not cease." (Gen.8:22)

Why would Jeremiah refer to a different covenant to the NHC, when it specifies that day and night will not cease? Do we actually read about a "covenant" with day and night in Genesis 1?[79]

In both cases, Isaiah 24:3-5 and Jeremiah 33:19-26, the context is tied to the world, to the earth, and to the NHC. This explanation will not satisfy GW, for their contention is that the NHC alludes to the AC, and, therefore, the NHC establishes the AC. But any presence of allusions to Genesis 1-2 do not demonstrate a *covenant* with Adam. If the presence of allusions is the criterion, then we would have to say that NC is actually the establishing of the MC, for there are many allusions to the MC within the NC.

A 'Silent Covenant'?

GW say that the word "covenant" does not have to be present in Genesis 1-2 for a covenant to be there. They write that "king" does not appear in Isaiah 66:1 but it is implied. Likewise, " "Torah" implies covenant as its reflexive".[80] Others tell us that God's relationship to David is not explicitly called a covenant in 2 Samuel 7 (see 1 Chr.17), but some time later it is called a covenant in Psalm 89:3, 28, 34, 39; Psalm 132:12; and Jeremiah 33:21. In conclusion, there is no mention of a "covenant" in Genesis 1-3, yet the theology of a covenant is present, so we ought to conclude that there is, indeed, a 'covenant' in the text.

As to the argument from silence (the 'silent covenant') itself, ultimately, it stands only if there are covenantal terminology and theology in Genesis 1-3. This particular sub-section deals with terminology, the next

---

[79] Carl F. Keil and Franz Delitzsch, *Biblical Commentary on the Old Testament: Jeremiah, Lamentations, vol.II*, transl. James Kennedy, (Edinburgh, UK: T. & T. Clark, 1874.), 74.

[80] Gentry and Wellum, *Kingdom Through Covenant*, 178.

handles theology. The weight of redemptive history is pressing against an AC precisely because in Scripture a covenant is expressed through covenant terminology such as "covenant", "oath," and so forth. Certainly, Yahweh's kingship is implied from Isaiah 66:1, yet that is due to the word "throne." Our record of covenants in the OT is inextricably tied to the use of the term *berit*. GW pendantically illustrate this point, for their lexical analysis of *berit* stretches to over sixty pages.[81] Due to this overwhelming evidence, one can readily identify covenant terminology and themes that surround *berit*. What is the specifically 'covenant' *terminology* that GW can cite from Genesis 1-2? Stephen Williamson refers to "the non-usage of covenant vocabulary before Genesis 6:18".[82] This is overstated. GW could cite the word "bless" (Gen.1:22, 28; 2:3). But what about "curse", or "oath", or other covenantal terms? In other words, there is not a grouping of covenantal *terms* that is indicative of the presence of a covenant. Nor do GW help their case by maintaining, " "Torah" implies covenant as its reflexive". Maybe this is so (see Gen.26:5); maybe it is not. Why is "torah" not used in Genesis 6-9 to reflect the NHC? Is there a reason why "torah" is used only once in Genesis? Regardless, if "torah" is a covenantal term it is identified as such due to the proximity of covenant terminology. For example, in Genesis 26:3, it states that God "will confirm the oath" he "swore", and "bless" Isaac-all familiar covenant terminology. Therefore, with John Murray I agree that the absence of the term "covenant" in Genesis 1-3 is a strong indicator that no covenant is present.[83]

Covenant Elements in Genesis 1-3?

---

[81] Ibid., 717-778.
[82] Williamson, *Sealed with an Oath*, 57.
[83] John Murray, *Collected Writings 2*, 50.

To understand if there are 'covenant' elements present in Genesis 1-3, it is imperative to define what a covenant is. However, GW are hesitant to define a covenant, but write:

> ...for heuristic purposes the following may be used as a place to start. 'an enduring, binding obligation(s) specified on the part of at least one of the parties toward the other, made by oath under the threat of divine curse, and ratified by a visual ritual'....[84]

A covenant shapes and gives direction to already existing relationships, just like a marriage does.[85] A covenant has oaths and bonds.[86] What was normally involved in making a treaty in the ANE? "Four features characterize this treaty, and, in fact are normative of covenants in general":

1. A covenant does not necessarily initiate a relationship; a relationship might already be in place before the making of a covenant.
2. There is conventional language for initiating a covenant, such as "to cut a covenant".
3. "A covenant gives binding and quasi-legal status to a relationship by means of a formal and solemn ceremony."
4. "Covenant making involves a commitment or oath or promise and frequently signs or witnesses."[87]

This is enough information about GW's definition of a covenant to work with.

---

[84] Gentry and Wellum, *Kingdom Through Covenant*, 132.
[85] Ibid., 155.
[86] Ibid., 59.
[87] Ibid., 152.

Even a cursory comparison between Genesis 1-2 and GW's criteria for a covenant expose the frailty of their argument.

✓ A previous relationship.
✗ No language of covenant initiation.
✗ No formal and solemn ceremony.
✗ No oath, or promise, or sign.

I am not aware that GW contest these omissions, and it is possible that the first criterion, a previous relationship, is not properly met. GW blur definitions. Their belief is that the act of creation itself was an instance of covenanting, for "covenant is essential to the being of God."[88] GW do not give a theological justification for this hugely important statement, other than to say that it has to be so because God created all things via a covenant with creation.[89] Of course, a CT reader will be yelling at GW, telling them to take it back one step further in time to conclude that there was an eternal covenant of redemption (after all, God was making a relationship with the elect in Christ). Yet, I am not aware that CT will be bold enough to declare that 'covenanting' is an attribute of God, even though this is required if covenanting is indeed *essential to the being of God*. Moreover, to maintain that the very act of creation by God is an act of covenant entails that relationships are inherently covenantal, since we are all creatures of God and covenanting is essential to the being of God. This teaching is obviously contradictory, for one cannot *make* a covenant with someone if being-in-relationship is expressive of covenant. GW respond to this criticism by saying that all covenants have a prologue in which the pre-covenant relationship of the two parties is outlined.[90] What GW have

---

[88] Ibid., 179.
[89] Ibid., 21, 179.
[90] Ibid., 180.

done is move the goalposts: to defend against the criticism that there are relationships that pre-date covenants, they have said that such relationships are recorded in a covenant document. Even so, the history in the prologue of a covenant becomes covenantal history only when the two parties agree to a covenant; up until that point, there is no covenant, "Rather than establishing or framing such a divine-human relationship, a covenant seals or formalizes it. The biblical order is relationship, then covenant; rather than covenant, hence relationship."[91] GW cannot have their cake and eat it.

I suspect one of the reasons GW are reluctant to define a covenant is because of the problems a purely definitional rendition of covenant presents when reading Genesis 1-2. Whether they feel it necessary or not, their evidence for a covenant in Genesis 1-2 has to rely upon a non-definitional approach, one that describes in a general sense covenantal elements. For example, God's commands to Adam are assumed as proof of the covenant and evidence of the major party in the covenant imposing the rules of the covenant.[92] In response, we can say that, God commands demons but he is hardly in covenant with them! Another supposed element is the language of curse and blessing is present. Man is blessed because God commanded man to be fruitful and multiply and to rule over the earth and its creatures (Gen.1:22, 28). And, there is a curse, for God says in the day man eats of the tree of the knowledge of good and evil he will die (Gen.2:17). Yet, there is no promise held out to man for obedience to God's command. Many assume that if Adam had obeyed, he would have been rewarded with eternal life. This turns on its head the thrust of Genesis 1-2. Contextually, there is no need to posit a reward. Adam was 'alive', spiritually alive, before the Fall. *This must be so for*

---

[91] Williamson, *Sealed With an Oath*, 75.

[92] Gentry and Wellum, *Kingdom Through Covenant*, 216.

him to die physically and spiritually! Why, then, introduce the notion that he would have received the reward of eternal life had he obeyed? Is it not more accurate to think he would have been confirmed in the *form of divine life* that he already had?[93] John Murray comments, "The race has been confirmed in sin, condemnation, and death by Adam's trespass. Surely this principle of confirmation would have been applied with similar consistency in the direction of life in the event of obedience on Adam's part."[94] Nor was the tree of life a symbol or sign of a covenant. Nor as GW say, was the tree of life promissory.[95] Life was at the very heart of Adam's existence before the Fall. It is often said that Adam did not eat from the tree of life. Yet, why should we conclude this? Did he not have life? Was he refusing to eat from all the trees? Even if he did not, was not man alive before the Fall? And, more to the point, was he not forbidden from eating from the tree of life *because he had sinned* against God and had *cast away* divine life (Gen.2:17; 3:22-24)? All in all, the absence of specific covenantal elements is abundant evidence that no covenant is present.

Has this lack of evidence made GW over-reliant on upon ANE covenantal models? I appreciate the work GW have done distinguishing between the suzerain and the royal charter models.[96] I also understand, to a degree, their unwillingness to accept the traditional conditional vs unconditional division.[97] Which kind of covenant is Genesis 1-2? It is a mix of conditional and unconditional, suzerain and royal charter. Of course, the suzerain model is

---

[93] That confirmation might have taken the form of praise from God and the expulsion of Satan.

[94] Murray, "Adamic Administration," 49.

[95] Gentry and Wellum, *Kingdom Through Covenant*, 667.

[96] Ibid., 133.

[97] Ibid., 279, 610.

not applicable to God's eternal plan.[98] And, GW reject the CT view of a Covenant of Redemption. What GW do not ask, however, is whether it is appropriate to apply the models of postlapsarian covenants to a prelapsarian world. It is to be feared that the tail is wagging the dog, for the ANE covenant models are conveniently present in the prelapsarian world. Was not the basis of the ANE covenantal structure of suzerain over vassal predicated upon the suzerain subduing his *enemy*?[99] Underneath the royal charters was the same arrangement of suzerain and vassal; this allowed a vassal to call upon his suzerain to protect him in the land.[100] I conclude that, it is anachronistic to compare the prelapsarian relationship between God and Adam to the postlapsarian, covenant world.[101]

It is probable that GW place so much hope in ANE models of the covenant because, as they write, "*The key to correct interpretation*, therefore, is to compare and contrast the biblical text and the data from the contemporary cultures."[102] [italics mine] This implies that the reader and theologian cannot understand Genesis 1-2 properly without knowing the culture and religious background of the ANE.[103] With this presupposition, GW's reading of

---

[98] Ibid., 60.

[99] See, Jeffrey Jay Niehaus, *Ancient Near Eastern Themes in Biblical Theology* (Grand Rapids, MI: Kregel Publications, 2008), 56-82; *God at Sinai: Covenant and Theophany in the Bible and Ancient Near East* (Grand Rapids, MI: Zondervan Publishing House, 1995), 102-107, 145. The classic work on ANE covenantal structures was George Mendenhall's, *Law and Covenant in the Ancient Near East* (Pittsburgh, PA: Biblical Colloquium 1955).

[100] Hal Harless, *How Firm a Foundation: The Dispensations in the Light of the Divine Covenants* (New York: Peter Lang, 2004), 16-17.

[101] See Williams, *Sealed with an Oath*, 56.

[102] Gentry and Wellum, *Kingdom Through Covenant*, 193.

[103] For one example, out of many, of this problem, see Gordon J. Wenham's *Exploring the Old Testament*, which begins its section on Genesis 1-11 with ANE parallels to Genesis 1-11. [Gordon J. Wenham,

Genesis 1-2 inevitably takes them to models of the covenant outside of the Bible, which are then superimposed upon a chronological era (before the Fall) in which ANE covenants did not exist! I will say this: it does enhance biblical study to understand the cultural and religious setting of the biblical material; but to call a combo of ANE cultural knowledge and biblical data an interpretive *key* is going too far. In that setting, the biblical data is in partnership with the ANE model and looking to it for validation.

Yahweh the *Covenant* God?

GW consider it a 'slam dunk' argument for the covenantal nature of Genesis 1-2 that God is called the "LORD" from Genesis 2:4 on as this is his covenant name. Thus, when God created Adam, he did so as LORD, Yahweh, Adam's covenant God.[104] It seems an open-and-shut case. But, there are questions needing to be answered.

Is it proper to say that "Yahweh" is God's exclusive covenant name? Two things can be said. First, if GW are correct in their assessment that God is by nature a covenanting God, then every name of God will necessarily be a covenantal name, since God cannot express himself outside of a covenant. In that setting, to talk about a specific name that is covenantal is redundant. Second, if Yahweh is a covenantal name, and covenanting is essential to God's being, why is not "Yahweh" introduced from the moment of Genesis 1:1? Surely the God of the covenant with creation should mark himself out from the beginning as a covenanting God in his essence. Third, in Exodus 6:3, God was known to the fathers as *El Shaddai* ("God Almighty") and not as "Yahweh" (see Exo.3:6). Genesis

---

Exploring the Old Testament: A Guide to the Pentateuch (Downers Grove, Ill: IVP Academic, 2015), 9-18.]
[104] Gentry and Wellum, *Kingdom Through Covenant*, 180.

17:1 records that the LORD appeared to Abram as God Almighty. The name Yahweh, and knowledge of Yahweh, went all the way back to Genesis 2:4. He was not 'known' as Yahweh, however. As some scholars have argued, in Exodus 6:3 we are looking at the difference between superficially knowing God's *personal* name of "Yahweh", but not knowing the power of that personal name in a deep, *covenantal* manner.[105] Does this imply that "Yahweh" was not the only covenantal name? Was not *El Shaddai* a covenantal name, also?

Coming to the name "Yahweh," was it a *covenant* name of God before, and during, the time of the fathers? Or, was "Yahweh" the *unique* covenant name of the God of Israel? Some think so.[106] Yet, if we bind the identity of the name "Yahweh" to the *covenant* God *of Israel*, we irreversibly limit the origin of the name "Yahweh" to the Mosaic Covenant and loosen the title from its place in Genesis; and, in my opinion, in doing so, we open the door for something like the abominable JEDP hypothesis.[107] If the fathers did not "know" God as Yahweh (Exo.6:3), did

---

[105] See Walter C. Kaiser Jr., *The Christian and the Old Testament* (Pasadena, CA: William Carey Library, 1998), 66; *The Old Testament Documents: Are They Reliable & Relevant?* (Downers Grove, Ill: IVP Academic, 2001), 142.

[106] John MacArthur, *The MacArthur Bible Commentary* (Nashville, TN: Thomas Nelson, 2005), 110; William Dyrness, *Themes in Old Testament Theology* (Downers Grove, Ill: Inter-Varsity Press, 1979), 46; Walther Eichrodt, *Theology of the Old Testament*, The Old Testament Library, Vol.1, transl. J. A. Baker, (Philadelphia: Westminster Press, 1961), 178-205.

[107] It has to be said that Old Testament scholarship in general is beginning to turn against the Documentary Hypothesis. [E.g., T. Desmond Alexander, *From Paradise to the Promised Land: An Introduction to the Pentateuch*, 3rd ed., (Grand Rapids, MI: Baker Academics, 2002), 7-31; R. W. L. Moberly, *The Old Testament of the Old Testament: Patriarchal Narratives and Mosaic Yahwism* (Eugene, OR: Wipf and Stock, 2001); Kaiser, *Old Testament Documents*, 142-143.]

this mean that *El Shaddai* was the only available covenant name of God at that time? Or were there two covenant names? If Yahweh was specifically a *covenant* name, why does not Genesis point this out as the book of Exodus does? I am not asking if God was in covenant with mankind or in covenant with the fathers; I am inquiring if, during the time of the fathers- and before- the *name* "Yahweh" indicated One who was specifically *in covenant.* Yahweh God was in covenant with Noah and his seed, with mankind. But was "Yahweh" specifically the *covenant* name of Noah's God? I think it safer to say that "Yahweh" was the *personal* name of God, who was the One covenanting with Noah, for in the Noahic narrative Moses does not identify "Yahweh" as a *covenant* name.

Even if this assessment is flawed, it raises problems for GW's understanding of the purpose of the name "Yahweh." Is "Yahweh" first and foremost a covenant name? If it is, then we are back to GW's assertion that God is inherently covenantal. Yet, "Yahweh" was used long before any citation of a 'covenant' (Gen.2:4ff.; Gen.6:18). I am not saying "Yahweh" is not used as a covenant name. Even so, all of God's names express something special about God; and it is most likely that "Yahweh" conveys an intimate and personal relationship between the Creator-God and man.[108] That is why it is taken up from Genesis 2:4 on and specifically applied to the narrative detailing man's creation. Likewise, the name is special to various generations because God is setting apart to himself a people, until, eventually, we come to the Israelites. It is then that God opens up his name "Yahweh" to his covenant people and they come to know him as the covenant One.[109]

---

[108] Robin Routledge, *Old Testament Theology: A Thematic Approach* (Downers Grove, Ill: IVP Academic, 2008), 83-84.
[109] See Allen P. Ross, *Recalling the Hope of Glory: Biblical Worship from the Garden to the New Creation* (Grand Rapids, MI: Kregel Academic and Professional, 2006), 146-148.

The response to this will be that Yahweh is the God of Israel, and that the use of "Yahweh" before Exodus 3 and 6 is Moses drawing attention to the fact that the covenant God of Israel is the Creator-God. However, if we leave matters like that, we surely miss the point and put the cart before the horse. The God of Israel, Yahweh, was the God of creation, of man, long before he was presented as the covenant God of Israel. The implication of this for Israel is that Yahweh, the God of man, will use Israel as a vehicle to bless mankind and not just Israel.[110]   When we study the name "Yahweh" in Exodus, the substratum of God's covenant relationship is evidently Yahweh's greatness as the Creator-God, his Lordship, and his sovereignty.[111] In Exodus 3:14-15, he is, in the first place, the God of the fathers, for Yahweh extends his roots beyond Israel unto the fathers. He is not, therefore, the God of Israel merely. W. Ross Blackburn, in referring to the greatness of God, says that the name Yahweh "declares the Lord's supremacy over humanity." When Moses objected that he did not speak eloquently, God roots the solution in the name "Yahweh", " "Who has made man's mouth? Or who makes him mute or deaf, or seeing or blind? Is it not I, the LORD?" " (Exo.3:11). Blackburn also says "Yahweh" indicates God's supremacy over nature. For example, in sending the plagues, God declared, " "I am the LORD" " (Exo.7:17; 8:22; cf., 8:10; 9:14, 29). This control over nature, says Blackburn, signifies that Yahweh is the Creator. "Yahweh" also refers to "the Lord's supremacy

---

[110] Cf., John Goldingay, *Old Testament Theology, Volume 2: Israel's Faith* (Downers Grove, Ill: InterVarsity Press, 2006), 30.
[111] See Walter Brueggemann's very detailed description of these aspects. [Walter Brueggemann, *Old Testament Theology: An Introduction* (Nashville, TN: Abingdon Press, 2008), 23-120.]

over other gods" (Exo.12:12).[112] Therefore, Yahweh's protection and care for his covenant people, Israel, issues from *Yahweh's prior status* as God, Creator, and supreme Lord.

In conclusion, there is no evidence that before Genesis 6, "Yahweh" was a specifically covenantal name. It was, rather, the name God used to identify personally with mankind. Only during the time of Moses did it become specifically a *covenant* name.

Hosea 6:7: Adam and a Covenant?

By taking recourse in Hosea 6:7, GW wish to silence critics who say there is no explicit evidence for an AC found in Scripture, "But like Adam they have transgressed the covenant; there they have dealt treacherously with me." GW's argument from Hosea 6:7 is that the phrase *keAdam* ("as Adam") most naturally refers to Adam the historical figure. Hosea 4:4-6, in allusion to Exodus 19:6, describes the sins of Israel's priests who have broken the MC. This is then connected with Adam's status in the Garden as God's priest-king. Hosea 6:7 reflects a parallel between Israel's priestly violation of the MC and Adam, as priest-king, breaking the AC.[113] However, this reading is reaching and assumes what it sets out to prove.

Coming to the context of Hosea 6:7, GW argue that *sham* ("there") is locative (see Hos.9:15; 12:4), but its referent may be "indirect". What do they mean by that? They write, "The phrase "like Adam" in Hosea 6:7 indicates sin in a place, the garden of Eden. The "there" can refer back to those circumstances." GW cite Hosea 9:9 and 10:9 as parallels:

---

[112] W. Ross Blackburn, *The God Who Makes Himself Known: The Missionary Heart of the Book of Exodus*, NSBT, ser. ed. D. A. Carson, (Downers Grove, Ill: Apollos, 2012), 41-44.

[113] Gentry and Wellum, *Kingdom Through Covenant*, 217-219.

> Since the days of Gibeah, you have sinned, Israel,
> and there you have remained.
> Will not war again overtake
> the evildoers in Gibeah? (Hos.10:9)

> They have sunk deep into corruption,
> as in the days of Gibeah.
> God will remember their wickedness
> and punish them for their sins. (Hos.9:9)

This reading is unsustainable, however, for it conflates a person and place: *adam* the person and the Garden. They are forced into this error because they believe *sham* is locative and anaphoric, it would seem. To say the least, this is a very creative reading of the text.[114]

This is not to deny that the meaning of Hosea 6:7 is a tough, if not impossible, nut to crack. Let me begin with the argument that *adam* indicates a place. Many scholars say that Hosea 6:7 denotes the town of Adam, which is cited in Joshua 3:16. Sometimes the preposition k^e (k^eAdam) is conjoined with a place, as in, "as Jerusalem" (*kiyrusalim*) (Song 6:4), so that one does not need to translate k^e as if it were b^e. Therefore, the preposition k^e ("as") conjoined with "Adam" can just as easily point to a place. "As Adam" would then denote the town Adam referred to in Joshua 3:16, and would implicate the whole of the town called Adam in breaking a covenant. The

---

[114] Coming to the same conclusion as GW, Bryon G. Curtis cites numerous word-plays and puns in Hosea. However, what Curtis is never able to do is show how one word can mean, at one and the same time, a person and a place. Like GW, it would seem that Curtis is pressed into this confusion because he believes the immediate and natural referent of *sham* is *adam*, a geographical place. [Bryon G. Curtis, "Hosea 6:7 and Covenant-Breaking like/at Adam," *The Law is not of Faith,* 197-207.]

presence of *sham* ("there") usually indicates a place, and contextually Adam seems the likely referent. In addition, other places are mentioned in Hosea 6:8-9 and this bolsters the interpretation that *adam* is a town. Some scholars think that because Adam, the town, and Gilead are in the same trans-Jordan area that Adam is in Gilead.[115] Yet, geographical referents of *sham* in Hosea, Micah, and Amos precede *sham*, so that the referent is most likely not Gilead.[116] In objection to this reading, there is no record of covenantal treachery committed at the town called Adam. Joshua 3:16 is about a great victory for Israel, as it is on the verge of taking the Promised Land. Consequently, the verse has nothing to do with Israel's sin. Some have suggested that behind Hosea 6:7 is perhaps the assassination of King Pekahiah by Pekah (2 Kg.15:25).[117] If there is a connection between the death of Pekahiah and a covenant, it is impossible to discern.[118] Which type of covenant was "transgressed" (see 2 Kg.18:12; Jer.34:18)? Was it the Mosaic Covenant that was violated at Adam? Was it the priestly covenant (Num.25:10-13; see Hos.6:9)?

Some writers opt for the view that *adam* refers to man in general. The LXX supports this reading (*anthropos*). The Israelites had broken the MC just like other men (Gentiles) who sin and break covenant. Robert L. Reymond considers this an "inanity" because there is no other way to break the covenant than as 'men'.[119] The thought is far from being inane. Israel was meant to be separated to Yahweh, but it behaved as mere "man", like

---

[115] Gary V. Smith, *The NIV Application Commentary: Hosea, Amos, Micah* (Grand Rapids, MI: Zondervan: 2011), 120; J. Andrew Dearman, *The Book of Hosea*, NICOT, (Grand Rapids, MI: Wm. B. Eerdmans Publishing, 2010), 198.

[116] Curtis, "Hosea 6:7," 196.

[117] Dearman, *Book of Hosea*, 198.

[118] See Curtis, "Hosea 6:7," 196.

[119] Robert L. Reymond, *A New Systematic Theology of the Christian Faith*, 2nd ed., (Nashville, TN: Thomas Nelson, Inc., 1998), 430.

the Gentiles (see Psa.82:7). This is not to say that Gentiles discarded the MC; but perhaps they broke some covenant made with Israel, similar to Solomon's covenant with Hiram (Amos 1:9; 2 Sam.5:11; 1 Kg. 5:1, 12; 9:13). Or, as in Isaiah 24:5, perhaps the Gentiles had broken the laws of the everlasting covenant, that is, the NHC (Gen.9:5-6). The same combination of *kaph* and *adam* is present in Job 31:33, " "Have I covered my transgressions like man (*k^{e}adam*), by hiding my iniquity in my bosom" (see Isa.43:4; Jer.32:20).

In response to the understanding that *adam* means mankind, some CT theologians cite Job 31:33 in support of their reading. However, as Byron G. Curtis, a CT theologian concludes, outside of Genesis, the only certain example of the name of the historical person Adam is found in 1 Chronicles 1:1.[120] Even so, the 'mankind' reading has to face the force of the adverb *sham*, "there". GW and Curtis consider it locative and non-temporal. If so, one cannot sensibly conclude that *adam* is either a person or mankind generically. However, if *sham* were read temporally, it is possible that it might link with Adam the person or with mankind. The NET bible feeds into such a possibility. It indicates that there are nonlocative and deictic uses of *sham*, interpreted as "then", "behold", or "see" (Psa.36:12; 48:7; 66:5; 132:17; Zeph.1:14), or as the NET Bible interprets *sham* in Hosea 6:7, "Oh how".[121] The irony is that the NET bible interprets *adam* as a place and not a person or mankind: "At Adam they broke the covenant; oh how (*sham*) they were unfaithful to me!" Is there anything to prevent, then, the reading, "As Adam, they broke the covenant; oh, how they were unfaithful to

---

[120] Curtis, "Hosea 6:7," 188-189.
[121] "Hosea 6:7-11," *Net Bible,* http://classic.net.bible.org/passage.php?passage=Hosea+6:7-11, accessed 5/22/2018.

me", or the reading, "As man, they broke the covenant; oh, how they were unfaithful to me"?

Although I cannot say with any confidence what the proper interpretation of Hosea 6:7 is, I can comment with a measure of confidence that the view that concludes that *adam* must indicate Adam the person is as exegetically suspect as the other two stances.

Non-Redemptive Covenants?

GW do not address the issue of whether divine covenants are inherently blood bonds, as Robertson maintains.[122] I assume that they do not accept his definition of a covenant. GW's method in interpreting Genesis 1-2 is to exegete it for parallels between the personal and relational God of creation and the personal covenant God of Israel, Yahweh. The God of Israel was a personal and covenanting God, so the God of creation, who is Yahweh, was a personal and covenanting God.[123] By doing this, GW homogenize OT covenants and epochs in history, identifying them with grace and covenant loyalty at the expense of the possibility that these epochs and covenants are not entirely harmonious. It is rather convenient for GW, however, that the AC does not have a blood ritual, for it is arguably so that the other divine covenants do incorporate blood and sacrifice.[124] Thomas Schreiner maintains that a divine covenant cannot be administered in blood, because there are too many covenants that contain no element of blood and sacrifice; for example, Jacob and Laban's covenant (Gen.31:44-54); Jonathan and David's covenant (1 Sam.18:3-4; 20:8, 16-17; 22:8; 23:18); marriage (Pro.2:17; Mal.2:14); Solomon and Hiram (1Kg.5:12); and Israel and

---

[122] Robertson, *Christ of the Covenants*, 4.
[123] Gentry and Wellum, *Kingdom Through Covenant*, 177-222.
[124] Robertson, *Christ of the Covenants*, 17-52.

the Gibeonites (Josh.9:3-27).[125] Schreiner makes a valid point. If words are to carry their proper meaning, it is advisable not to say that *all* covenants are 'redemptive', for the concept of redemption is that of deliverance and setting free someone, and this value is not evident in every biblical covenant.[126]

To be fair, Roberston is defending the nature of *divine* covenants, not all covenants. Yet, I think he is scratching at something that is characteristic of all biblical covenants. We might ask, why covenants? This is what it all boils down to. As to the AC, GW seem more concerned about its form and its presence in Genesis 1-2 than asking about the 'why' of the supposed AC. Not all covenants may be founded on blood, but they all signify the need to protect a relationship and to establish peace and unity. That is, there is a sense in covenants of something being fixed or protected from danger. There was nothing needing protection, or fixed, prior to the Fall. Peace and unity were not necessary, for they were already present. There was no need to 'seal the deal', for sin and division were not an ever-present danger. Why did the Gibeonites covenant with Israel? The Gibeonites were afraid of being wiped out by the Israelites (Josh.9:3-15). Jacob and Laban were not BFFs, to say the least, and to make the peace between themselves, they created a covenant (Gen.31:25-32:55). David and Jonathan covenanted with one another to demonstrate their mutual love and that they would not harm

---

[125] Thomas Schreiner, *Covenant and God's Purpose for the World*, Short Studies in Biblical Theology, ser. eds. Dane C. Ortlund, Miles V. Van Pelt, (Wheaton, Ill: Crossway, 2017), 14-18.

[126] Hebrews 9:16-17 is written in the context of contrasting the covenant of Moses with the new covenant in Christ Jesus. Thus, *diatheke* does mean "covenant." [For a full argument, see Allen, *Hebrews*, 477-482.] Both these covenants were founded upon blood. Therefore, it is more likely that, the writer of Hebrews is not saying that every covenant was founded upon blood, but that the two main divine covenants were.

each other. That is why Jonathan disarmed himself and gave his weapons as a pledge of their covenant (1 Sam.18:1-5). Solomon and Hiram made "peace" with one another and thereby made a covenant (1 Kg.15:12). And why a covenant for marriage? Does not the context of Proverbs 2:17 tell us? Is it not because of the grave danger of going after an adulterous woman (Pro.2:16-19)? And Malachi 2 teaches us that God is a witness against divorce and disrupting a marriage (Mal.2:14-16). Therefore, although covenants were not redemptive, they were applied to protect and preserve a peaceful relationship from disintegration and trouble, from 'enemies' to that relationship. Therefore, it is apparent that the missing factor in GW's rendition is that covenants deal with potential divisions in relationships and the need to consolidate peace.

A covenant became necessary after the Fall due to the disintegration of relationships: man's relationship with God; male with female; man with the animals; and, man with the earth. Due to sin, God later introduced covenants. Before the Fall, the first couple was not in covenant, for there was nothing broken that needed fixed, nothing that needed protection from sin and division.

However, a covenant was not instituted directly after the Fall, yet, the promise was. For, at the end of the day, it is all about the promise and not about the covenant *per se*. The covenant is a means to an end: it preserves the promise, and to the extent that the covenant preserves the promise is the covenant indispensable. This relationship between promise and covenant is drawn out by the contrast between the Abrahamic Covenant and the MC. The latter was to highlight sin; it was not created to protect the promise. Whereas, the Abrahamic Covenant was (Gal.3:15-17). The Abrahamic Covenant therefore prevailed as a covenant, but the "Law" brought a ministry of death and condemnation and slavery (2 Cor.3:4-9; Gal.4:21-31). The promise of Genesis 3:15 precedes the covenant, of any kind, including Noah's covenant. The promise ensured man's victory over the Serpent through the Seed of the woman. However, the old Adamic 'man', the seed of the Serpent, was driven by the 'un-image', the broken-down image of Adam that was polluted by sin. It was that un-image, a totally depraved soul, that led to the murder and lust and grab for power expressed in Genesis 6:1-6, that, in turn, led to God wiping out mankind, except a few elected ones. It was then God said he would establish a covenant, for if man was left to himself, he would wipe himself out! Thus, a 'high-perimeter security fence' was set around *this* original covenant to protect the human race from both wiping itself out due to the malevolent presence of the curse, sin, evil, death, beasts, and Satan and from God's consuming wrath.

In conclusion, as Williamson correctly identifies, defenders of an AC must broaden the definition of a covenant to incorporate the scenario set before us in Genesis 1-2, but in doing so they devalue the elements of a covenant found elsewhere in the OT.[127] In other words, GW's common-denominator approach removes the specific purpose of a covenant, its 'why'.

The last exegetical argument to look at is the parallel between Adam and Christ.

Adam and Christ: Two Covenant Heads?

GW cite the parallelism between Jesus and Adam found in 1 Corinthians 15:21-22 and Romans 5:12-19. Both men are covenant heads and represent those who are united to them. Adam disobeyed, so he brought sin and death upon mankind. Jesus obeyed, so he brought righteousness and life upon the church.[128]

---

[127] Williamson, *Sealed with an Oath*, 58.
[128] Gentry and Wellum, *Kingdom Through Covenant*, 616-618.

The parallelism between Christ and Adam is undeniable, but they are not paralleled covenantally. It is abundantly obvious from Romans 5:12-21 and 1 Corinthians 15:21-22, 45, 47, that Adam is negatively contrasted to Christ and not positively compared to him. Adam brought sin and death; Jesus gave us righteousness, life, and immortality. Also, in the NT when covenant contrasts are made they are between Moses and Jesus, not Jesus and Adam (2 Cor.3; Gal.3:17; 4:21-31; Eph.2:11-21; Heb.7:22; 8:6-13; 9:1, 4, 15, 18, 20; 10:16, 29; 12:24; 13:20). Search as you will, you will look in vain for an explicitly covenantal connection between Christ and Adam. Moreover, Paul had an opportunity to insert covenant language into the setting of Romans 5:14 when juxtaposing Adam to Moses, yet Paul compared Adam, the man of the command, to Moses as the man of the Law. GW maintain that because the NT calls Adam "son of God" (Luke 3:38) and a "type" of Christ (Rom.5:14), descriptions that are not aligned with Adam in the OT, then it is fair to assume that Adam was in a covenant, too, for he obviously reflects Christ, the Image of God.[129] The same counter-reply is suitable here as put earlier: Scripture *does* refer to Adam as a type and *does* call Adam "son of God", but Scripture does *not* say Adam was in a "covenant."

'But Christ was in covenant with his people!' Yes, he was, but that was because he had to redeem them. Before the Fall, Adam had no need to redeem anyone, so no covenant was necessary. It is safe to assume that every reference comparing Adam to Christ in the NT may be read as contrasting the role of the failed head of creation, Adam, with the covenantal head of the church, Jesus Christ, who came to redeem his people.

Was not Satan, the Serpent, a threat? Does this not entail that there was a need for a covenant, therefore, before

---

[129] Ibid., 195, 196, 397, 398, 641.

the Fall? Covenants assume the prior presence of evil within the actual life of the system and the need to reverse evil's course. Covenants therefore restrain, unite, protect, in that sense. The earth and its order was perfect; there was no sin anywhere. There was no need for a covenant, therefore.[130] Satan was not part of the order of earth: man, the creatures, and the plants. Satan was a being from an alternative place, an extraterrestrial being, literally; he was a deceptive intruder, and he was not part of the fabric of earth and its order. After the Fall, all kinds of evils were let loose on mankind and were now entrenched in the world's nature. God's relationship with Adam was focused upon this world and its creatures, and not upon the invisible world and its beings. This 'earthly' relationship between Adam and the LORD is, as I will soon show, set against the advanced spiritual nature of Christ's covenantal relationship to the Father and the immortal and heavenly nature of the life from above.

Having responded to the exegetical evidence put forward by GW for an AC, we move on to a critique of hermeneutical factors lying behind their understanding of Adam and the AC.

---

[130] A similar counter-argument is made concerning marriage: if marriage is a covenant, why is it not labelled as such in Genesis 2? This is proof that a covenant does not need a label to be present in a text- so the argument goes. This logic, once more, assumes that the conditions before and after the Fall are identical. It is typical of CT to flatten the eras and epochs out as if sin does not exist! Man before the Fall was united to woman. There was no need for a covenant because the union between man and woman was perfect. After the Fall, there was a dire need to protect this union from all kinds of evil.

3.

A HERMENEUTICALLY SUSPECT VIEW OF ADAM AND THE AC

GW make the AC the hermeneutical key for all other covenants. If the covenants are "foundational" to the metanarrative of Scripture,[131] then the foundational covenant of all the others is the AC, "the main point is this: the "covenant with creation" and Adam's representative role in the covenant is *foundational* to all the biblical covenants."[132] [italics mine] Thus, the AC is the 'foundation of the foundation,' the epicenter and engine of GW's covenantal-metanarrative thesis.

In essence, what GW have done is drawn a straight line of continuity from the so-called AC to the NHC onto all the other covenants. This is the flattening effect I spoke of earlier. It is a positive view of the AC and not a negative reading of it. The positive Adamic model GW employ reaches its covenant terminus in Jesus Christ, who is the last in the series of Adams, the Last Adam, and who "recovers the original situation", which is to say, he recovers the AC bringing it to its proper end (*telos*) and fulfillment.[133]

Now, if the AC is the heart of GW's thesis, the heartbeat is the belief that after the Fall God hung on to mankind because of his covenant commitment to the

---

[131] Gentry and Wellum, *Concise Biblical Theology*, 17.

[132] Gentry and Wellum, *Kingdom Through Covenant*, 617.

[133] Ibid., 120, 124, 617, 631, 714, 716.

human race. Sin disrupted God's original purpose, got man kicked out of the Garden of Eden, but sin did not destroy God's purpose, so he persevered with man.

In contrast to GW's 'hermeneutic of Adam (the first man),' my thesis is that subsequent to the Fall, the Adamic administration (for there is no covenant) is destroyed; however, by his grace, God preserved mankind, when he could have destroyed them due to their sin. God persevered with mankind *solely* out of his grace and mercy, so that he might fulfill his plan of redemption. Consequently, the presence, or 'continuity', of the themes of the Adamic administration in the rest of the bible is due to God seconding, or utilizing, the categories of the original administration to bring about his promise of salvation that is eventually fulfilled in Jesus Christ. In that setting, the typology and themes of the Adamic administration that are present in the OT do not arise out of the need for covenant fulfilment or because of a covenant obligation, but because God in his mercy has a *new* purpose for mankind, one which is stated in the *protoevangelium* and that utilizes the older categories described in the Adamic administration.

In this light, the negative ramifications of GW's Adamic thesis are immediate. First of all, GW underestimate man's sin and the Fall.

GW Underestimate the Centrality
of Man's Sin and the Fall

Let me underscore their problem with a question: could God have sent Adam and Eve directly to hell for their sin? Due to the controlling principle of a covenant, and the positive value GW put on Adam and his headship, it would seem that they would have to answer that question in the negative. GW have mistaken God's patience and mercy to Adam and Eve, as recorded in Genesis 3:14-24, as a commitment to some unspoken promise or covenant given before the Fall. Why does God send anyone to hell if he has to honor his covenant with *mankind*? Even if one does belief in an AC, it does not follow that after the Fall, God still had a purpose for mankind *within that original covenant*:

> Q.20. Did God leave all mankind to perish in the estate of sin and misery?
> A. God having, out of his mere good pleasure, from all eternity, elected some to everlasting life, did enter into a covenant of grace, to deliver them out of the estate of sin and misery, and to bring them into an estate of salvation by a redeemer.[134]

The Westminster Shorter Catechism is right to draw attention to what could have happened to man had not God's grace immediately intervened. CT theology posits the Covenant of Grace of Genesis 3 that takes over, so to speak, from the Covenant of Works (Adamic Covenant). And whilst I do not accept an AC or a Covenant of Grace, nonetheless, CT has captured the dire need for a major change in God's plan for creation (from a human point of view) due to the presence of sin.

GW's Thesis Makes the *Protoevangelium* the Handmaiden of Covenants Theology

This problem flows out of the previous one. In the positive Adamic climate GW create, Genesis 3 and the promise concerning the Seed of the woman are placed on the periphery, yet pushed to the fore is covenant continuity and

---

[134] "Westminster Shorter Catechism with Proof texts" *Center for Theology and Apologetics* (n.d.),
http://www.reformed.org/documents/wsc/index.html?_top=http://www. reformed.org/documents/WSC.html, accessed 6/2/2018.

faithfulness. That is why, in GW's *God's Kingdom Through God's Covenants*, in the chapter, "The Covenant with Creation in Genesis 1-3", Genesis 3 itself is allotted two-thirds of a page, with a couple of comments later in the book.[135] KTC fares the same, for in the chapter, "The Covenant with Creation in Genesis 1-3", there is no discussion of the implications of the *protoevangelium*. In fact, the role of Genesis 3, in that chapter, is as a source for supporting data derived from GW's exegesis of Genesis 1-2. Later in KTC, roughly ten pages are given over to a discussion of the effects of Adam's sin recorded in Genesis 3 and to the *protoevangelium*.[136] It is readily apparent, therefore, that in GW's system, the *protoevangelium*, rather than being given the proper attention it deserves as the starting point of redemption history, is considered as a stepping stone in a covenants-dominated theology.

The reader might dispute my assessment here and express the view that GW do adhere to the *protoevangelium* as the starting point of redemptive history. It is equally plain, the reader might say, that GW do adhere to a historic Fall and to the ruination of man's life due to Adam's sin.[137] I accept these comments. But, it is the place these facts have, and their significance, within GW's hermeneutic that I am challenging. The *protoevangelium*, indeed its surrounding context of promise, is quickly passed over in pursuit of the covenants. To be pointed, a hermeneutic of continuity in the covenants pushes out a hermeneutic flowing *from the promise*. So, I must insist that, in GW's system the *protoevangelium* and its context is merely an insertion into, a stepping stone toward, the grander scheme of the fulfillment of covenants.

GW's AC is Built upon a Faulty

---

[135] Gentry and Wellum, *Concise Biblical Theology*, 91, 257, 258.
[136] Gentry and Wellum, *Kingdom Through Covenant*, 618-628.
[137] Ibid.

Interpretation of Covenant Loyalty

Why do GW insist that a broken, discarded relationship with man, that was made in Eden, is still applicable today? They think so because of their conception of God's covenant loyalty: God will always honor and fulfill his covenants, and because of that, he will restore mankind to the glory it should have had via Adam. Followed through to its logical terminus, this view entails that not only the AC, but all other OT covenants, must be restored (for all the 'minor' OT covenants are organically one with the AC).

Bearing this in mind, one can argue that the MC is not old, rather, the NC merely renews the Old. Ironically, this is the position that GW come very close to advocating. In reading GW, we hear the crisp sound of the ending of the MC:

> But in the text itself, he is saying that the future restoration for Israel and the gift of other peoples to Jerusalem will come about not on the basis of the Israelite covenant at Sinai but instead on the basis of the Abrahamic covenant. The Israelite covenant was broken, but the Abrahamic covenant still stands.[138] ...the covenant with Israel *as a whole covenant package* comes to its end and Christians are no longer under it *as a covenant.*[139] [italics theirs]

So, the contrast is between a covenant that still stands and one that does not; one that is broken and one that is live. But then GW state that in ending the exile of Israel, God "renews the covenant" with Israel, and that God is

---

[138] Gentry and Wellum, *Concise Biblical Theology*, 220.
[139] Gentry and Wellum, *Kingdom Through Covenant*, 635.

"restoring the covenant relationship".[140] Where does it say in Isaiah 54:1-55:13 that God "renews" the *Mosaic* Covenant? "Through the covenant at Sinai he married Israel and so is her husband, and now he is the redeemer, i.e., the nearest relative, who has the duty to buy her back from exile and slavery."[141] GW write concerning Isaiah 54:6:

> God will now show [Israel] compassion, mercy, and covenant loyal love forever. The marriage relationship will be *restored*. There will be a new covenant, called a covenant of peace in verse 10 to emphasize the fact of reconciliation. God's anger has been appeased and finished. Israel may now benefit from the healing of a broken relationship in a new covenant. *The new covenant renews and restores the broken old covenant.* But it is more than that. It is a new covenant, different from the old one and superior to it, because it depends not upon God's people but instead upon the everlasting kindness of God himself.[142] [italics mine]

Earlier, I speculated that GW's thesis of *heqim berit* and *karat berit* could be taken to the extreme of maintaining that a covenant might be, at one and the same time, a new covenant and an old covenant. In GW's comments above, we observe that exact phenomenon. How can God restore the MC with Israel, yet discard it at the same time? How is the NC completely new, yet it "renews and restores the broken old covenant"? If a craftsman 'restores' a piece of

---

[140] Gentry and Wellum, *Concise Biblical Theology*, 210, 211.
[141] Ibid., 214.
[142] Idem. See, *Kingdom Through Covenants*, 423.

furniture, he is not making a brand-new piece of furniture; he is merely restoring something that is old, making it look new. GW tell us, quite correctly, that the opening of Isaiah 54, in verses 1-3, envisages the influence of the *Abrahamic Covenant*.[143] It is this covenant, the NHC, and the Davidic Covenant (Isa.55:3), I submit, that are influencing the NC teaching of the prophets. Thus, in Isaiah 54:4-10, the emphasis is not upon the 'restoration' of the covenant with Israel, but upon God re-marrying Israel. GW misapply a simple fact: that a new marriage means a new covenant. God divorced Israel, yet he was going to marry her again. New marriage = new covenant, *not* the restoration of the old covenant, or marriage, that he originally had with Israel. There is not the slightest indication that God is restoring that which was old. The old failed, completely. Israel who will be re-married is qualitatively different, because she will be established in righteousness (Isa.54:14), and their relationship to God is qualitatively different because he will never again cast-off Israel.

GW then discuss what is new about the NC. This is part of their answer:

> The new covenant restores the broken relationship between God and Israel by bringing the forgiveness of sin....
>
> Fourth, the expression "I will cut a new covenant" (*karat berit*) shows that God is not simply affirming the Sinai covenant or renewing the Sinai covenant; he is initiating or inaugurating a new covenant.[144]

This seems perfectly reasonable NCT. But let us complete the quote:

---

[143] Gentry and Wellum, *Kingdom Through Covenant*, 441-442.
[144] Gentry and Wellum, *Concise Biblical Theology*, 234, 235.

Fourth, the expression "I will cut a new covenant" (*karat berit*) shows that God is not simply affirming the Sinai covenant or renewing the Sinai covenant; he is initiating or inaugurating a new covenant. This automatically renders the Israelite covenant obsolete as *a code or formalized agreement*. Recall that the Israelite covenant is both a law treatise and a covenant or vassal treaty. A *new arrangement or code* will be put in place between God and his people, *but the instruction in the code will be the same*. As a result, when we compare old and new covenant, we can say that we are not bound to the old covenant *as a code*, but that *righteousness of God demonstrated in the old covenant has been enshrined and incorporated into the new*.[145] [italics mine]

In saying these things, GW are trying to preserve a line of continuity between the MC and the New. But, why not say that the MC was made obsolete *as a covenant*, as the NT states? Why stress its 'code' nature? It is not a new arrangement or code that is put in place between God and Israel, but a new *covenant*. We are not bound to the MC *as a covenant*. And since when did the MC demonstrate God's *salvific* righteousness? Is it not the case that the MC demonstrated an impossible righteousness, one of works? And is not the teaching of the NC entirely different to the old, Mosaic, Law? Do not Christians observe the law of Christ?[146]

---

[145] Ibid., 235.
[146] Gentry and Wellum, *Kingdom Through Covenant*, 635-639; A. Blake White, *The Law of Christ: A Theological Proposal* (Frederick, Md: New Covenant Media, 2010).

The reason why GW cannot seem to make their mind up is because of their definition of divine covenants. They are, by their nature, expressive of his "covenant loyal love forever".[147] Simply put: God cannot give up on his covenants. *That is why GW cannot give up on the AC and its continuing relevance as the foundational covenant of covenants.*

GW's Thesis Makes Adam a Positive Role-model for the Covenants

Due to their insistence on covenant continuity from creation onward and their definition of a covenant, GW have to make Adam a positive covenant figure. The reader will be tempted to think that I am thoroughly mistaken and hamming the issue, for positive allusions to Adam and the prelapsarian order are throughout Scripture. I am not denying the allusions to the Adamic administration. Rather, I dispute the so-called inherent positive value set upon *Adam* and the Adamic administration. *Is there really a positive model of Adam in the OT?* Looking beyond Genesis 1-2, the Seed is the new *Ish* ("male"); indeed, the term "seed" (*zera*) in Genesis 3:15 indicates a male. From a canonical perspective, we know that male as Jesus Christ. This is contrasted to Adam who failed.[148] That is why

---

[147] Gentry and Wellum, *Kingdom Through Covenant*, 423.

[148] Abner Chou, *The Hermeneutics of the Biblical Writers: Learning to Interpret Scripture* (Grand Rapids, MI: Kregel Academic, 2018), 84-86; Jared M. August, "The Messianic Hope of Genesis: The Protoevangelium and Patriarchal Promises," *Themelios* 42:1 (2017): 46-62; T. Desmond Alexander, "Messianic Ideology in the Book of Genesis," *The Lord's Anointed: Interpretation of Old Testament Messianic Texts*, eds. Philip E. Stterthwaite, *et. al.*, (Eugene, OR: Wipf and Stock Publishers, 1999), 19-40; Jim Tunstall, *The Seed of the Woman: The Story of an Ancient Prophecy Fulfilled* (Bloomington, IN: AuthorHouse, 2011); Eugen J. Pentiuc, *Jesus the Messiah in the Hebrew Bible* (New York: Paulist Press, 2006); Sandra King, *Adam*

Adam is never put forward in the Old or New Testament as a positive figure. It is no coincidence that the Flood narrative is packed with references to "man" (*adam*) failing (Gen.6:1, 2, 3, 4, 5, 6, 7; 7:21, 23; 8:21; 9:5). It is because *adam* is such a rotten failure that Noah sacrifices to God to appease him (Gen.8:21), and it is due to *adam* and the animals remaining evil that God has to impose an extreme sanction in his very first covenant, for he declares that man (*adam*) or animal shedding the blood of *adam* will require the blood of the offender (Gen.9:5-6).[149] Consequently, *adam* is not set apart in Genesis as a positive figure, and in the place of *adam* is the promised Seed of the woman. In this context, if we come back to the historical Adam, even if Hosea 6:7 is a citation of Adam in covenant the verse declares that he failed miserably.

This Adam sits in sharp contrast to the true Seed, the true Adam. Herman Witsius comments:

> Christ is the seed of Adam, whose son he is called, Luke iii. 38.; also the seed of Abraham, and the Son of David....Yet there was great reason why he should be here [in Genesis 3:15] called the seed of the woman, rather than of Adam. For Adam, in scripture, is represented as the origin of sin and death....Wherefore he who delivers us from sin and death, ought not to be considered as subordinate to Adam, and as his son: but, as the second Adam, and the head of another family, opposed to Adam....Adam, as he was the origin of sin and death, is opposed

---

and the Woman: A Prophetic Picture of Christ and His Bride (Maitland, FL: Xulon Press, 2008), 86.

[149] The irony is thick here: man and the animals are equal in evil and depravity. This, of course, links us back to Genesis 3 and the Evil one who inhabited the serpent.

to Christ; as himself was saved, is to be accounted to the seed of the woman, whose head is Christ, and so to be subordinate to Christ. Christ therefore is called the seed of the woman, because, being the origin of a better stock, he is opposed to Adam as the root of a corrupt race.[150]

When we come to the NT, the same model of negativity applies. As already shown, GW draw a straight line of covenantal continuity between the First and Second Adams. I wish to concentrate on 1 Corinthians 15:45, 47. There we read about Jesus, who is the antitype of the Adam of Genesis 1-3 and the fulfillment of the son of man of Psalm 8 (see ahead). Jesus is the "last" or eschatological Adam, the fulfillment and antithesis of the Adam who brought death to men (1 Cor.15:22). Jesus is also the "second" Man. He is not the third, or fourth, or fifth. He is the second. There have only ever been two Adams and not a sequence of little Adams: one from the earth, and his antithesis from heaven:

> [47] The first man is from the earth, earthy; the second man is from heaven. [48] As is the earthy, so also are those who are earthy; and as is the heavenly, so also are those who are heavenly. [49] Just as we have borne the image of the earthy, we will also bear the image of the heavenly (1 Cor.15:47-49).

The difference is between heaven and earth, the Adam from above and the Adam from below. To Paul's mind, Jesus is not in a straight line of continuity with historical Adam, for

---

[150] Herman Witsius, *The Economy of the Covenants Between God and Man: Comprehending A Complete Body of Divinity*, vol.2, transl. William Crookshank, (London: R. Baynes, 1822), 117.

Jesus as the Man for us is from heaven, whereas, Adam belongs to the sod.

The straight line of continuity from Adam to Christ is also destroyed by the nature of both Adams, and it is this distinction that brings us to the very nub of the debate over an AC. According to 1 Corinthians 15, Adam's body was perishable, dishonorable, weak, natural, and from the earth (vv42-44, 48-49). We, too, in our bodies bore the image of earthy Adam (v49). In sum, " "The first MAN, Adam, BECAME A LIVING SOUL" " (v45). Verse 45 is crucial, for it tells us the limits of Adam's nature. His "glory" (vv35-41) was a limited glory, one which gave way to perishability, etc.. To be specific, his "life", *which was a divine life*, was one specially crafted by God to excel in this world that we now know as earth. Thus, Adam was from the earth and not from heaven. His body was not imperishable, immortal, and heavenly. His glory was not from heaven (1 Cor.15:42-49). Adam's body and life were pre-eschatological and natural; Christ's body is eschatological and spiritual.[151] John Calvin writes:

> Paul makes an antithesis between this living
> soul and the quickening spirit which Christ

---

[151] See Richard B. Gaffin, *Resurrection and Redemption: A Study in Paul's Soteriology* (Phillipsburg, NJ: Presbyterian and Reformed Publishing Company, 1987), 78-85. Scholars go too far when they posit that if Adam had obeyed the LORD, he would have inherited eschatological life and Sabbath, or received an immortal body like Christ's. [Cf., Meredith G. Kline, K*ingdom Prologue: Genesis Foundations for a Covenantal Worldview* (Eugene, OR: Wipf Stock, 2006), 78, 91-117; Lee Irons, "The Sabbath as an Eschatological Sign of the Covenant," *The Mountain Retreat: Center for Biblical Theology and Eschatology* (n.d.), http://www.mountainretreatorg.net/eschatology/the_sabbath_as_an_esc hatological_sign.shtml, accessed 6/4/2018; G. K. Beale, *A New Testament Biblical Theology: The Unfolding of the Old Testament in the New* (Grand Rapids, MI: Baker Academic, 2011), 262.]

confers upon the faithful, (1 Corinthians 15:45), for no other purpose than to teach us that the state of man was not perfected in the person of Adam; but it is a peculiar benefit conferred by Christ, that we may be renewed to a life which is celestial, whereas before the fall of Adams man's life was only earthly, seeing it had no firm and settled constancy.[152] Moses relates that Adam was furnished with a living soul; Christ, on the other hand, is endowed with a life-giving Spirit. Now it is a much greater thing to be life, or the source of life, than simply to live.[153]

And, Richard Gaffin insightfully observes:

In Romans 5:12-21 (and 1 Corinthians 15:21-22), the contrast is between Adam of Genesis 3, the fallen sinner, and Christ as righteous; Adam's death-dealing transgression stands in opposition to Christ's obedience and reconciling death (vv.5-10, esp.10). In 1 Corinthians 15:45-49, this contrast, already sweeping enough in Romans 5, is even broader, between Adam as *created*, the Adam of Genesis 2 before the fall, and Christ as resurrected, the bearer of the resurrection, eschatological life, as

---

[152] John Calvin, *Commentaries on the First Book of Moses Called Genesis*, transl. John King, (Edinburgh, UK: The Calvin Translation Society, 1847), 112-113.
[153] John Calvin, *Commentary on the Epistles of Paul the Apostle to the Corinthians, vol. II*, transl. John Pringle, (Edinburgh, UK: The Calvin Translation Society, 1849), 52.

life-giving Spirit in the sense of the Holy Spirit....

....The order of Paul's outlook here is such that Adam is "the first" (*ho protos*, v.45); there is no one *before* him. Christ is "the last" (*ho eschatos*); there is no *after* him; he is literally the *eschatological man*.[154] [italics his]

In that respect, Adam reflects the same subordinate, inferior, nature that Moses does according to 2 Corinthians 3:9-11:

> [9] For if the ministry of condemnation has glory, much more does the ministry of righteousness abound in glory. [10] For indeed what had glory, in this case has no glory because of the glory that surpasses it. [11] For if that which fades away was with glory, much more that which remains is in glory.

The MC was inherently weak and had an intrinsically inferior glory. Likewise, the first man was inherently weak and possessed an inferior glory, *even in his state of innocence.*

To be specific, as originally created by God, Adam was created as one who could, potentially, die, sin, and turn against God. It was an earthy, of this world, image and life. Had Adam obeyed God, the result would not have been immortality, for it, and other such blessings won by Christ for his church, belong to the heavenly world and not this terrestrial globe. Nor am I referring to postlapsarian Adam,

---

[154] Richard Gaffin, *By Faith, Not Sight: Paul and the Order of Salvation*, 2nd ed., (Phillipsburg, NJ: P&R Publishing, 2013), 53.

but to prelapsarian man.[155] Put another way, it is not merely that heaven and God and the risen Messiah are the source, from heaven, of the church's blessing of eternal life. Rather, the salvation we possess, in all its shades and hues, is distinctly heavenly, expressing the very character of God himself (2 Pet.1:4; Heb.12:10; 1 John 3:2; John 6:31-58). This salvation is in no way tied to this earth, this world, or man's original makeup; nor is immortality and glory the logical terminus of anything on earth, such as a theoretical Adam who successfully negotiates the test of the Garden. The nature of salvation is that it is the life of heaven, *of God*, eschatological life, given to wicked man who has been pardoned in Jesus Christ.[156] This is eschatological life that will be fulfilled in heaven coming down to earth, to redeemed man. At the center of this eschatological life is God himself, who will be the temple (Rev.21).[157]

---

[155] Gerald Bray extends this principle to say that in his innocence Adam was not only non-immortal, he was mortal by nature and would have eventually died. [Gerald Bray, "Adam and Christ (Romans 5:21-21)," *Evangel* (Spring, 2000): 5-6.] I do not think that the one follows the other. Certainly, Adam was not immortal. Yet, he was not mortal in the sense of possessing a life in his body that would *necessarily* eventually vanish. Prelapsarian Adam was a unique figure, so that his physiological and spiritual makeup were one-of-a-kind. Throughout Scripture, the entrance of death is tied to the entrance of sin (I am not going to rehearse that argument). To posit an underlying reason for the existence of death outside of man's sin requires an extensive BT investigation of the matter, and Bray does not offer this up.

[156] P. T. O'Brien, "The Church as a Heavenly and Eschatological Entity," *The Church in the Bible and the World: An International Study*, ed. D. A. Carson, (Eugene, OR: Wipf Stock Publishers, 1987), 88-119; Mark Goodwin, *Paul, Apostle of the Living God: Kerygma and Conversion in 2 Corinthians* (Harrisburg, PA: Trinity Press International, 2001), 222-230; Larry Hurtado, *The Lord Jesus Christ: Devotion to Jesus in Earliest Christianity* (Grand Rapids, MI: William B. Eerdmans Publishing Company, 2005), 373; Beale, *Biblical Theology*, 591; Richard Gaffin, *Resurrection and Redemption*, 78-97;

[157] George Eldon Ladd, *A Theology of the New Testament*, rev. ed., ed. Donald A. Hagner, (Grand Rapids, MI: William B. Eerdmans

Yet, was not Adam called the "son of God" in Luke 3:38, and was this not in a line of continuity with Jesus? The genealogical line set out in Luke 3:23-38 is prophetic and selective in nature. We are taken back to prelapsarian Adam before he fell. There is no inherent value in Adam's prelapsarian status, for man has ruined the original image. However, Scripture invests the prelapsarian era with prophetic quality, so that the former- yet defunct-administration prophetically points beyond itself to its fulfillment in the Son of God. If Luke were recapitulating the AC and prelapsarian Adam then the line of heritage would come from Cain, the firstborn, and not Seth. However, as Adam's 'divine' sonship is held up as a prophetic symbol, it follows that the lineage that extends from Adam to Christ is one that is based on the promise. (For the same method, see my comments on Genesis 5.) For that reason, Luke 4:1-13 goes immediately to the true Son of God who defeats Satan and overcomes the test of God in the wilderness. Jesus' genealogy, in Luke 3, draws out merely his human side, for he proceeds from Adam, and is called the son of Joseph. Jesus is the true Son of the Most High God (Luke 1:32, 35), the King (Luke 1:32-33) and the salvation of Israel, the light of the Gentiles (Luke 2:30-32), the One who was greater that John the Baptist and who will baptize with the Spirit (Luke 3:16).

Having completed my critique of GW, I will briefly describe, and give examples of, an alternative model for interpreting the 'Adamic' imagery of the OT.

Publishing Company, 1993), 522; Dave Matthewson, *A New Heaven and a New Earth: The Meaning and Function of the Old Testament in Revelation 21.1-22.5* (Sheffield, UK: Sheffield Academic Press, 2003), 195.

4.

'ADAMIC' IMAGERY SEEN THROUGH THE EYES OF THE PROMISE

To GW the matter is straightforward: where there are elements of the prelapsarian order, there we have an allusion to the AC and its reassertion and eventual restoration. Thus, every 'Adamic' text becomes an immediate proof-text.

The Basic Pattern

The counter-model I work with is that which places the *protoevangelium* and the promise at the heart of interpretation. Adam has fallen and his administration and mankind with him. His image, *although it still exists*, is a bust. Yet, God spared mankind from utter ruination, and merely according to his grace held out hope to him in the form of the promise of the Seed. By faith in the promise of the Seed, believers come to share in a new image (or at least its OT version).[158] Consequently:

> ➤ The OT is no longer interested in Adam, his image, or his administration.

---

[158] NCT advocates will say that this cannot be so, for we receive the image of Christ in the NC era. I agree. It is not the image of Christ *per se* that Noah and all OT believers received; it was, rather, a seminal, promissory version of this NC image. That is, they looked forward by faith in the promise to the new image of God in Christ the Son.

➢ His image is busted and now exists in the whole of mankind as an 'anti-image' or 'un-image.' That is, mankind utilizes the broken image against God and function as rebels.[159]

➢ The various sections of Scripture that use 'Adamic' language and imagery do not do so out of loyalty to that administration, but because God uses that imagery and language in a *prophetic* manner to point mankind toward the Seed of the woman, who represents a new image and a new creation.

➢ Thus, God seconds and utilizes the world of the Adamic administration and the Adamic image, temporarily sanctifying them for his own purpose, to bring to pass the fulfillment of the promise concerning the Seed and the true, heavenly image.

➢ The new creation and new image do not share in the image of Adam; the new image is not a restoration of the original image anymore than Christ's resurrection body is a restoration of his *earthly* body. To 'restore' means merely bring back to its original luster. Christ's resurrection body, and ours, belong to a new world. A new world demands a *new* man with a *new* image. That is why Christ and his image belong to the *New* Covenant.

---

[159] Too often it is thought that because man still has the original, Adamic, image, that this image must be something that does not change and is exactly the same in Christian and non-Christian, and exactly the same in Adam before the Fall and in humanity after the Fall. This would mean, however, that something in man was not tainted by sin. This I cannot accept, and if it were accepted it would be a modern form of Socinianism. The basic categories, or specs, of the image are the same before and after the Fall. Therein lies the element of continuity. But all these specs, or functions, are turned to an evil purpose, for they have been infiltrated by sin. Or, as Calvinists would say, man is *totally* depraved.

➤ For these reasons, the NT invariably describes Adam in a negative, and not positive, manner as the symbol of sin, death, and failure.

In presenting this model, I limit my examples to six texts as a sampler: Genesis 3:15 and its context; Genesis 4; Genesis 5; the NHC; the Abrahamic Covenant; and Psalm 8. Some texts utilize 'Adamic' imagery, and others (Genesis 3:15; Genesis 4; and Daniel 7) focus on the prophetic nature of the new and promised Man.[160]

Genesis 3:15 and Context[161]

---

[160] I am currently in the process of writing a book that uses NCT principles and the model stated in this book to describe the theme of the image of God in Scripture.

[161] I am assuming a traditional evangelical interpretation of Genesis 3:15. Therefore, the notion that Adam was not a historical figure is dismissed. [*Four Views on the Historical Adam*, gen. eds., Michael Barrett, Ardel B. Caneday, (Grand Rapids: Zondervan, 2013), 89-254.] So also is the naturalistic reading of Genesis 3:14ff.. [Cf., Sigmund Mowinckel, *He That Cometh: The Messiah Concept in the Old Testament & Later Judaism*, transl. G. W. Anderson, (Grand Rapids, MI: William B. Eerdmans Publishing Company, 2005), 11.] Mowinckel writes, "man tries to crush the serpent's head when he has a chance"! [p.11.]] It ignores the supra-natural factors present in the text: a speaking animal; the entrance of the powers of sin, death, and the curse which were anything but natural; the presence of a non-earthly being (whom we later came to know as Satan) who indwelt the serpent; and, the Seed will defeat this malicious 'being' by crushing his head; consequently, the Seed must be more than natural. [See, Jared M. August, "The Messianic Hope of Genesis: The Protoevangelium and Patriarchal Promises", *Themelios* 42:1 (April 1, 2017): 54.] Also, the view that says Genesis 3 does not teach a fall of mankind is rejected, too. [See Hans Madueme, "Rumors of Adam's Demise: One More and Counting," *The Gospel Coalition* (March 17, 2017), https://www.thegospelcoalition.org/reviews/adams-genome/, accessed 6/13/2018; cf., Dennis R. Venema and Scot McKnight, *Adam and the Genome: Reading Scripture after Genetic Science* (Grand Rapids, MI: Brazos Press, 2017).]

The collective nature of the seed (*zera*) implies one who represents the collective many. This seed, an individual and collective 'head', will strike the head of the Serpent. [Michael Rydelink, *The Messianic Hope: Is the Hebrew Bible Really Messianic?*, NAC Studies, ser.. ed., E. Ray Clenenden (Nashville, TN: B&H Academics, 2010), 140; August, "The Messianic Hope of Genesis", 53-56.] Some recognize this corporate leader but reject any connection between him and the Messiah. [John H. Walton, *et. al.*, *The NIV Application Commentary*, Kindle edition, (Grand Rapids, MI: Zondervan, 2015).] Yet, it is most likely that John develops this imagery and brings the "woman" into her full expression as the Messianic community that birthed the Messiah. [G. K. Beale, *The Book of Revelation: A Commentary on the Greek Text*, NIGTC, (Grand Rapids, MI: William B. Eerdmans Publishing Company, 1999), 678.] Moreover, Romans 16:20 patently alludes to Genesis 3:15 and is applied to the church- a church that has Jesus Christ as its head.

Recently, certain evangelicals have taken to reasoning that suffering, death, and evil were present in the world before the Fall. They note that the Serpent was slithering around and that woman's pain will increase during childbirth. If her pain increases, it implies that she could have experienced pain before the Fall. [Ronald E. Osborn, *Death Before the Fall: Biblical Literalism and the Problem of Animal Suffering* (Downers Grove, Ill.: InterVarsity Press, 2014.] Various versions and commentators agree with the interpretation, "I will great increase your pain in childbirth" (Gen.3:16). I do not think it is correct. The first clause in Hebrew most naturally reads, " "I will greatly multiply your toil and conception" " (הַרְבָּה אַרְבֶּה עִצְּבוֹנֵךְ וְהֵרֹנֵךְ). The repetition of *rabah* implies that multiplication will happen to the nth degree. The verb is a play on its use in Genesis 1:22 (x2), 28, where it refers to the multiplication of birds and then the multiplication of man. The noun *itstsabon* ("toil") is used in the next verse, Genesis 3:17, to refer to man's struggle with the soil. Likewise, in Genesis 5:29, the noun indicates "toil" ("toil *of our hands*"). In other words, *itstsabon* never indicates sorrow, emotion, or pain. Woman's role in creation was to give birth. She had circumvented her role by eating from the tree of the knowledge of good and evil. Now woman will not only have to bear children, but it will be a most burdensome and difficult task. Thus, the second clause of verse 16 expresses that woven into that burden is pain (בְּעֶצֶב תֵּלְדִי בָנִים). [Kenneth Matthews, *Genesis 1-11:26: An Exegetical and Theological Exposition of Holy Scripture*, The New American Commentary, vol.1A., (Nashville, TN: B&H Group, 1996), 249-250; Carol L. Meyers, "Gender Roles and Genesis 3:16 Revisited," *The*

I said previously that although GW acknowledge the reality of the centrality of the *protoevangelium*, in practice they do not give it a central place. We must, therefore, give the *protoevangelium* its proper position. Walter C. Kaiser brightly comments:

> The "seed/offspring" mentioned in [Genesis 3:15] became the root from which the tree of the OT promise of a Messiah grew. This, then, was the "mother prophecy" that gave birth to all the rest of the promises. Charles Brigg agreed: Genesis 3:15 was "the germ of promise which unfolds in the history of redemption."[162]

Genesis 3:15 and its context is the *prophetic matrix* that re-births the Adamic administration's language and imagery. The Adamic administration and its image no longer is an end in itself, but it is seconded and utilized by the promise to bring about God's salvation through the Seed of the woman. So, two things stand out: *first, the old order is a dead end; subsequently, the old order prophetically points toward something greater than itself.*

Word of the Lord Shall God Forth: Essays in Honor of David Noel Freedman in Celebration of His Sixtieth Birthday, eds., Carol L. Meyers, M. O'Connor, (Winona Lake, IN: Eisenbrauns, 1983), 344-345.] It is then that the Lord lays on woman the third stricture on her waywardness: she will desire her husband and he will rule over her (Gen.3:16c). Thus, there is no indication that pain was present in the pre-Fall era. Death was a most unnatural event, and the ambience of Genesis 1-3 precludes the notion of death being present before the Fall.
[162] Walter C. Kaiser, Jr., *The Messiah in the Old Testament* (Grand Rapids, MI: Zondervan Publishing House, 1995), 37-38.

The Seed of the woman is a male, and in that regard, he takes over from where Adam left off.[163] *Therefore, we are no longer looking to Adam, as all eyes are fixed on the Seed.* Adam was a man of the sod, created from the sod. The Seed has the attributes that make him a man that surpasses the original template in Adam. The Seed will overcome the Serpent and his seed. The Serpent (the serpent possessed by a creature not belonging to this world, later known as Satan) was the bearer of evil, whose guile let loose on mankind all non-earthly powers- sin, death, and the curse.[164] Consequently, the Seed simply could not be a mere man, one from the sod, one merely after the image of Adam, for that image was specifically crafted from, and for, this world, to have dominion over mere creatures of the earth and not over beings who did not belong to the 'natural' order. Nor could the image given to Adam conquer death, sin, division, and evil, for these, as stated already, were extra-terrestrial forces, that is, forces that did not belong to the original order, or nature, of the world. The implication is that the Seed comes with a new image, one that has the capacity and capabilities to destroy and overcome evil. We are now dealing with a whole other ball of wax, a totally different image- one which incorporates non-earthly power to defeat non-earthly forces. Nor is this a NT reading of the OT. It is joining the dots together in context, within Genesis 3.

The context of Genesis 3:15 explicates the above principles. We are told about the Seed of the "woman".

---

163 Jason S. DeRouchie, "Father of a Multitude of Nations: New Covenant Eschatology in OT Perspective," *Progressive Covenantalism*, 33.

164 God brought all the creatures before Adam (Gen.2:19-20). He intimately knew all the creatures, for he named them. He would have come across the serpent and naturally noticed how it, along with all the other creatures, did not talk. Thus, when the Serpent spoke, Adam and Eve would have known, intuitively, that the natural order was broken and some other, non-earthly, being was at work.

Man and woman, distinguished as male and female, belong to the old order of Adam. Yet, God uses this sexual distinction and their original roles to fulfill his greater, promissory, goal in the Seed. Thus, woman will give birth to a man, a male, a Seed, who will strike the head of the Serpent. In verse 16a, we are informed that God will give woman childbearing pains. Why? Well, of course, woman sinned and she was punished. But there is more to it than this. She is now bearing children in a context, *not primarily* of going into all the earth and populating it, but of providing a Seed who will crush the head of the Serpent. Her pain in childbirth is in accordance, of a piece, with the struggle that the Seed will go through to defeat the Serpent and his seed; for we know that to defeat the Serpent and his seed, the Seed of woman will be struck on his heel. This implies suffering and death.[165] Consequently, the woman's

---

[165] Bruce K. Waltke, *An Old Testament Theology* (Grand Rapids, MI: Zondervan, 2006), 266. Some reason that because the snake strikes at the foot of the Seed that there is no victory for either the snake or the Seed, for both receive mortal blows- one to the head and the other receiving poison to the foot. Consequently, we are told there is no note of hope in context. Then this is utterly amazing, for if there was no hope for man, why would God tolerate him? Also, why would God place woman against the Serpent (Gen.3:15), if there was no hope? Jared M. August maintains that the Seed struck a mortal blow, and the Serpent merely achieved a severe blow. [August, "The Messianic Hope of Genesis", 51.] There is a certain amount of 'joining the dots together' in the early chapters of Genesis, especially chapters 1-3. I think it likely that the Serpent strikes a mortal blow. We must bear in mind that the punishment for man's sin was death (Gen.2:17). The implication is that in pursuance of this judgment God will use the Serpent to execute his decree. However, the wider implication is that the Seed of the woman, via his death, offers hope to man, for he will crush the head of the Serpent. I think the key is this imagery. The idea is placing the foot on the head, a concept that probably images a victory for the one placing the foot on the other's head (see, Psalm 110:1; Rom.16:20). The head, in Scripture, is the place of authority. In context, woman is to submit to her husband, her head, who is in authority over her (see 1 Cor.11:10). In doing this, she will succeed

pain is not local, or earthly, the experience of every woman; this woman is the bearer of the Seed and so even her pain bears a prophetic nature, reflecting the struggle between her supra-natural offspring and evil, extra-terrestrial forces.[166]

Likewise, we are told in Genesis 3:16 that she will desire her husband and he will rule over her. I think it is most regrettable that this verse has been contorted to say, over the years, that man's rule will be overbearing and that woman will retaliate by desiring her husband's authority (but I do not have the time or space to get into that debate here).[167] As before, God is reasserting his old system-husband as ruler, wife as a helper, desiring her husband-

---

over the Serpent. Properly speaking, however, it is the Seed who brings victory; it is the Seed who is the true authority and head; his authority outpunches Satan's. Somehow, for we do not know at this early stage in Genesis, the death and authority of the Seed will crush the Serpent, his authority, and his enmity.

[166] See John H. Sailhamer, *Genesis*, The Expositor's Bible Commentary, gen. eds. Tremper Longman III, David E. Garland, Kindle Edition (Grand Rapids, MI: Zondervan, 2008).

[167] Not only does Genesis 1:26-28 imply man's headship as "man", and from Genesis 2 man's lordship over woman (for he named her), but Genesis 3:15 implies that man and woman will be victorious over Satan and at peace with one another. [Irvin A. Busenitz, "Woman's Desire for Man: Genesis 3:16 Reconsidered," *Grace Theological Journal* 7:2 (1986), 203-212; David J. A. Clines, *What Does Eve Do to Help? And Other Readerly Questions to the Old Testament* (Sheffield, England: JSOT Press, 1990), 36, 39-40; C. "John Collins, Adam and Eve in the Old Testament," *Adam, the Fall, and Original Sin: Theological, Biblical, and Scientific Perspectives*, eds. Michael Reeves, Hans Madueme (Grand Rapids, MI: Baker Publishing Group, 2014), 14-15.] Satan's strategy was to divide and conquer: he divided woman from man. Yet, here is woman, the source of the original sin, fighting back against Satan. If she is fighting him, she is not on his side. Nor is she duped by him. Consequently, she will not tempt her husband and draw mankind into sin and division. Obviously, the text is pointing to a relationship that transcends mere human relationships, to one that is steadfastly able to resist Satanic intrusion.

but in the context of the Seed defeating the Serpent and his seed. In other words, for woman to be successful (for Genesis 3:16 is addressed to the woman) and bear the Seed of victory, she will have to follow God's order and her husband's leadership. Once again, this is not an earthly, every-man, form of headship over woman; in Genesis 3:16, man's headship and leadership is in the context of redemptive history, properly speaking, and of the victory over the Serpent. As already noted, this is not a canonical reading merely, but is a legitimate extrapolation from Genesis 3. That being said, in 1 Timothy 2:11-14, Paul puts the same theology into its canonical setting:

> [11] A woman should learn in quietness and full submission. [12] I do not permit a woman to teach or to assume authority over a man; she must be quiet. [13] For Adam was formed first, then Eve. [14] And Adam was not the one deceived; it was the woman who was deceived and became a sinner. [15] But women will be saved through childbearing- if they continue in faith, love and holiness with propriety.[168]

What, then, of Genesis 3:17-24? It follows the same prophetic model set in verses 14-16. Certainly, man is being punished and he is kicked out of the Garden, so that we clearly see, yet again, that the Adamic administration in itself is a bust. However, man's struggle with the sod indicates, even symbolizes, man's struggle with the Serpent, for the source of the conflict with the soil is Satan himself; he is even the Serpent of the sod, for God cursed him to eat the dust (Gen.3:14), which is probably a sign of

---

[168] Francis L. Davis, *The Christian's Warfare: It's a Family Affair* (Xulon Press, 2008), 132.

God humiliating his enemy.[169] However, the ultimate failure of the prelapsarian Adamic order is that it does not prevent man returning to the dust from whence he came (Gen.3:19). Man by himself is bound to the sod. Yet, as before, this is in itself a signal that to overcome sin, the curse, and the Serpent, the Seed will have to overcome death. Also, by being kicked out of the Garden, man no longer can harvest it and receive life from the tree of life. That signifies that man will have to seek life from another source; but that has already been hinted at through the clothing of man's nakedness by animal skins. To sum up, the presence of Adamic categories is temporal due to the Fall and signifies the fulfillment of the spiritual promises of God centered upon the Seed of the woman. Thus, if we were to phrase Genesis 3:14-21, we would say, "Hope blossoming from punishment" (see Isa.6:13; Gal.3:14). And it is this hope, in the Seed, that the OT unfolds.

Genesis 4

We now move on to the narrative of Cain and Abel. Eve rejoiced that by the help of the LORD she had received a "man" (*adam*) (Gen.4:1).[170] Some think that Eve is offering up praise for receiving his help to bear a child. No doubt this is true, but it does not touch upon the prophetic implications of her comment. She probably anticipated that this "man" would be the Seed. This son was the firstborn,

---

[169] Gordon John Wenham, *Genesis 1-15*, WBC, vol.1, gen. eds., David A. Hubbard, Glenn W. Barker, (Waco, TX: Word Books, Publisher, 2017), 79.

[170] This text has been contorted in various ways due to critical theories of Genesis that functionally make extra-biblical sources equal in authority with Scripture. [Cf., John Byron, *Cain and Abel in Text and Tradition: Jewish and Christian Interpretations of the First Sibling Rivalry* (Leiden: Brill, 2011); J. T. A. G. M. Van Ruiten, *Primaeval History Interpreted: The Rewriting of Genesis 1-11 in the Book of Jubilees* (Leiden: Brill, 2000).]

had the rights of inheritance, and the LORD had helped her to bear the "man." All the ingredients for the coming of the Seed.[171] J. Ellsworth Kalas hits the nail on the head, "in this naming of Cain, Eve also seems to calculate that with this child she will get revenge of the serpent."[172] Yet, it was Cain![173] It is now apparent that Cain is the anti-man, the un-man, the one who, carrying the name "man", opposes God's *adam*. Cain is, not to put too fine a point on it, the seed of the Serpent (see John 8:44; Matt.22:33; 1 Jh.3:8; Matt.3:7-10; 12:34; 23:15, 28, 33).[174]

Genesis 5

Genesis 5 is a traditional go-to text that is said to demonstrate that the image of God after the Fall is the same as before the Fall. I reject this thesis (see my comments before on Luke 3:38). Adam's image is destroyed and in tatters (not removed entirely but broken beyond repair). Only through faith in the promised Seed does one participate in a promissory and inchoate fashion in a supra-natural image, one which foreshadows the heavenly image to come in Jesus Christ. At the heart of Genesis 5:1-2 and its citation of Genesis 1 is the prophetic promise of the Seed who bears the new image:

---

[171] Sidney Greidanus, *Preaching Christ from Genesis: Foundations for Expository Sermons* (Grand Rapids, MI: William B. Eerdmans Publishing Company, 2007), 92.

[172] J. Ellsworth Kalas, *A Faith of Her Own: Women in the Old Testament*, Kindle edition, (Nashville, TN: Abingdon Press, 2012).

[173] Commentators refer to the 'sibling rivalry' between Cain and Abel. There was no sibling rivalry, only sheer and total evil pouring out of Cain alone.

[174] Todd L. Patterson, *The Plot Structure of Genesis: 'Will the Righteous Seed Survive?' in the Muthos-Logical Movement from Complication to Denouement*, Biblical Interpretation Series, vol. 160, gen. eds. Paul Anderson, Jennifer Koosed, (Leiden: Brill, 2018), 67.

> This is the book of the generations of Adam. In the day when God created man, He made him in the likeness of God. [2] He created them male and female, and He blessed them and named them Man in the day when they were created.

Moses does not draw attention to the ruined image, so the Hebrew text stresses the phrase "in the day that" (*beyom*) to take us back to the day of the actual creation of Adam and Eve, to that time *before* the Fall and before the un-image. *Moses is looking back to the past to get his direction for the future.* That is, the LORD utilizes the imagery of the prelapsarian order to prophetically point us away from the Fall to the future and the coming Seed, to a new image, a new son, and a new world.

Scholars reason that because Seth was made in Adam's image, then Genesis 5:1-2 is a continuation of the teaching of Genesis 1:26-28. However, this subverts the prophetic nature of Genesis 5:1-2 and misunderstands why it is said that Seth was made in the image of Adam. If we had here a recapitulation of Genesis 1 and Adam as representative of mankind, the human line would follow Cain and his progeny as primary leaders of "man". Patently, Moses' concern is not prelapsarian man (who failed) but the *promise* as given to man and the promise as received by man (Gen.3:15), or to be more precise, part of man. I have maintained all along that God seconds, or utilizes, the original image in Adam to bring about his promise in his Seed. Adam is the first link in a *prophetic* lineage that is pushing us closer and closer to the Seed. So, the Seed will come from Adam and Eve *as believers*, through the line of Seth. That much we can say with certainty.[175] More to the point, why does not the text say that Seth was in the image of God? Why does Genesis 5 keep saying, "and then he died" (vv5, 8, 11, 14, 17, 20, 27, 31)? It was because he reflected his father and his *fallen image*; but, according to the promise, it was his line that God had selected to bring about the fulfillment of the promise.[176] Adam is not passing on a spotless prelapsarian image to Seth but his deadly image. Yet, Seth and his line have been selected by God to receive the baton of the promise that reflects a new image, one that is prophetically modelled in the *prelapsarian Adam and Eve*.[177]

Influenced by Genesis 3:15, the promissory nature of the lineage given in Genesis 5 is apparent. The same influence is behind the other genealogies of Genesis.[178] In the Hebrew world, the firstborn was foundational to a family's lineage. Yet, Cain is discarded. The 'new'

---

[175] John L. Thompson, ed., *Genesis 1-11*, Reformation Commentary on Scripture, (Downers Grove, Ill: IVP Academic, 2012), 216-218. *Contra*, R. Kent Hughes, *Genesis: Beginning and Blessing* (Wheaton, Ill: Crossway, 2005), 118.

[176] John Nicholas Lenker, *Commentary on Genesis: Luther on Sin and the Flood*, vol.2, (J. N. Lenker, 1910), 97; Paul F. Taylor, *Six Days of Genesis: A Scientific Appreciation of Chapters 1-11* (Green Forest, AZ: Master Books, 2009), 129.

[177] It is quite perplexing that commentators choose to specify that the original image of God was "tarnished" by the Fall. [E.g., Anthony A. Hoekema, *Created in God's Image* (Grand Rapids, MI: William B. Eerdmans Publishing Company, 1994), 15; James McKeown, *Genesis, The Two Horizons Old Testament Commentary*, gen. eds., J. Gordon McConville, Craig Bartholomew, (Grand Rapids, MI: William B. Eerdmans Publishing Company, 2008), 45; Ike Ijeh, *The Mystery of Godliness: Eternal Mysteries Explained* (Xulon Press, 2006), 68.] An odd choice of a descriptive. The writers are trying to balance out the idea, on the one hand, of the preservation and natural beauty of the divine image over against the pernicious effects of sin on the image. The offspring is this bizarre *tertium quid* of a 'tarnished' image. If I may break from character here to use urban language: the image got *rekt*!

[178] Chou, *Hermeneutics of the Biblical Writers*, 85.

firstborn is Seth. He is the firstborn *according to the promise.* Aside from Seth, the firstborn sons listed are, (Enosh (5:7); Kenan (5:10); Mahalel (5:12); Jared (5:16); Enoch (5:18); Methuselah (5:21); Lamech (5:25); and, last but not least, Noah (5:28). Like true sons of the promise, they are linked with piety. Noah was righteous and blameless and he walked with God (Gen.6:9). Most famously, "Enoch walked with God; and he was not, for God took him" (Gen.5:24). It is easy to miss part of Moses' point: Enoch has moved on to that realm, or sphere, where the image has its full spiritual value. If this earth was the final resting place for the image of the Seed, why did God not leave Enoch alone? We must recall, too, that Genesis 4:26 says that it was at the time of Enosh that men began to call upon the name of the LORD. Enosh was the son of Seth. In this, the text is moving beyond the original image and Adam and the earth, to a new Adam, a new garden, and a new image. Enoch was a beacon, a forerunner, who had shown the way to the LORD's presence and to fellowship with him.

Rather surprisingly, perhaps, in Yahweh's divine wisdom, he pitted one 'family' against another in piety, the lineage of the Seed's image against the lineage of the un-image. This is brought out by the replication of close-sounding names of the various firstborn (see figure 1 below):

Figure 1

Cain	Seth
Enoch (4:17)	Enoch (5:18)
Irad (4:18)	Jared (5:15)
Mehujael (4:18)	Mahalale (5:13)
Methushael (4:18)	Methuselah (5:15)
Lamech (4:19)	Lamech (5:25)

The numerous firstborn of the line of Cain are pitted against the enumeration of firstborn of the line of Seth. This is not a mistake. Both were immediate sons of Adam. Cain was the true firstborn, the first one born of the flesh. Seth, although he came from the flesh of Adam and Eve, was a son of the promise, in that he and his line pursued the faith of his mom and dad, Adam and Eve. There is no neutral lineage, and, therefore, no neutral category for the divine image. Nor is the divine image something that is impervious to sin and change. It was ruined in man by sin. *And even though it still exists*, it does so in a truly monstrous form (*ala* Cain and his seed). The *promised* image is *not* the restoration of the original Image; for the promised image is not based on natural birth as such, nor is it tied to this world, as Methuselah proved. The promised image prepares "man" for the world to come, for fellowship with God, to overcome sin, death, and Satan the Serpent. *It is crucial to see, therefore, that the citation of Genesis 1:26-28 given by Moses in Genesis 5:1-2 is entirely prophetic.*

The NHC

An obvious 'Adamic' theme is the Noahic mandate to go into all the world (Gen.9:1). GW draw a straight line from this datum to Genesis 1:28. Yet, so much has happened in-between. Man has sinned. Satan has entered the world. Death has eaten man's soul, and soon his body will feel its sting. In other words, now there are major unearthly forces controlling man that were not before the Fall. Man is now in a state of constant alert. But, there is hope in the promise, through the Seed. What is the true purpose of Noah and his progeny populating the earth? It is this, *they are meant to show the victory of God by subduing a world destroyed by sin*. Genesis 10-11 examine the different lineages of man coming from Noah to record what they did before God. Man was meant to spread out into the world, but the un-image prevented that from happening. Thus, even Noah's seed finally gives way to corruption. Sin and defiance- the old Satanic ways- have a firm grip on man.

The 'Adamic' language of Genesis 9 must be read in this context of the fight against this world and its fallen image. Noah, an individual, is given the charge by God as one representing many, a theme reflecting the influence of Genesis 3:15.[179] Thus, immediately following Genesis 9:1, we read that the fear and terror of man will be upon the animals, for not only will the creatures of the earth be food for man, but the beasts are now at war with man, threatening his very life (Gen.9:2-4). Although I reject the etiological, or naturalistic, reading of Genesis 3:15 that explains why men kill snakes, this does not take away from the spiritual struggle that started because of God pitting the Serpent and his seed against the woman and her Seed. Later, the Philistine Goliath threatened to feed David to the birds of the sky and beasts of the field (1 Sam.7:44). Israel could not enter the Promised Land in a single year because there were so many beasts in the land and they would multiply against Israel (Exo.23:29). When Yahweh restores Israel, he will make a "covenant of peace" that will "eliminate harmful beasts from the land", so that "beasts of the earth will not devour" Israel (Eze.34:25, 28). Thus, even the animals have been set against man: this is the implication of Genesis 3:14 that stated that the Serpent was cursed above the livestock and wild animals. Later in Scripture, the wild animals come to figuratively represent God's enemies (Isa.56:9; Jer.12:9; Dan.4:28-37; 7; Eze.34:5; Mark 1:13; see Jer.27:6; 28:14). Yet, this had already been fulfilled by the prediluvian world of men. They were beyond evil (Gen.6:1-7, 11-13). And we can go

---

[179] Idem.

back further yet, to Adam who behaved as though he were a son of the Serpent, the follower of Satan.

It has got to be the case, then, that the image of God has utterly changed. Could the original Adamic image subdue sin, stop death, control the beasts, and reverse the curse? Yet, this new image is 'gunslinging', for it packs heat and attacks the enemies of man, which include man himself and the animals (Gen.9:6-7).[180] This is to say that, the original image might still be present, but it is not an end in itself; *as a failure, it points beyond itself* to an image that succeeds against supra-natural forces and overcomes the beasts, death, man, Satan, and sin in the world.

Maybe Noah is the promised Seed. Certainly, his dad thinks so (Gen.5:29), and Noah looks like 'the man', the Seed, for mankind is wiped out and we are left with Noah and his seed (Gen.9:9). Yet, he is another 'son of the sod' (Gen.9:20). Noah falls flat on his face, literally, sloshed out of his mind with his own wine (Gen.9:20-24). Also, one of his sons is evil, so Noah curses Ham's son, Canaan (Gen.9:20-25). Why does Noah fail? He fails because he carries Adam's image, the original father. It is death within him. Yet, as a failure for the candidate *for the Seed*, he directs us away from himself to the Seed *to come*. Or, if I may, the Adamic imagery of the prelapsarian world is taken up by Moses to describe the redemption that will come through the promised Seed, or the *Second* Adam. It is not prelapsarian Adam in himself who is a positive role model, therefore; it is the Seed, for he is the Adam who will deliver mankind.[181]

The Abrahamic Covenant

---

[180] Although it is the divine will that man and beast be punished for killing man, it is man himself that God will use to bring to bear retribution.

[181] Greidanus, *Preaching Christ from Genesis*, 13; Waltke, *Old Testament Theology*, 299.

Abram is told he will be great and God will bless him and the peoples of the earth through him (Gen.12:2-3). 'Abram is a second Adam', we are frequently told.[182] Is this right? This, as we saw, was GW's interpretation.

It is incorrect, however. If prelapsarian Adam is the prototype, why is his name never connected with the covenant heads? The so-called 'Adamic' comparisons in Genesis 12:2-3 do not indicate that God is restoring the Adamic administration.

- Was God going to make Adam a great nation?
- Did God say he would make Adam's name great?
- Did God say he would bless those who bless Adam?
- Did God say he would curse those who curse Adam?
- Did he say that all the people of the earth would be blessed through Adam?

Now, the reader might answer in the affirmative to some of those questions, but not all of them.

It is not prelapsarian Adam and his time that is held up as the foundation of the Abrahamic covenant, but the promise of the Seed is the focus. The Abrahamic covenant is concerned with his blessed seed (Gen.15:3, 5, 13, 18; 16:10; 17:7, 8, 9, 10, 12, 19; 21:12, 13; 22:17, 18). Like Genesis 3:15, Moses once again uses the singular *zera*: the one represents the many.[183] August concludes:

> Just as God promised Adam and Eve, God likewise promised Abraham that his "seed" will…destroy evil (defeat the serpent

---

[182] C. John Collins, *Did Adam and Eve Really Exist?: Who They Were and Why You Should Care* (Wheaton, Ill: Crossway, 2011), 68.
[183] Chou, *Hermeneutics of the Biblical Writers*, 85.

through the "seed" of Abraham- 22:17b-18)....Therefore, in view of the anticipatory nature of the first promise of the Bible as well as the record of how the patriarchs understood this promise, one cannot help but appreciate Genesis 3:15 as the *protoevangelium*.[184]

Psalm 8:4

'What, then, about Psalm 8 and the "Son of Man (*adam*)" (Psa.8:4)? Is this not based upon a positive line of continuity between the prelapsarian era and the time of Psalm 8?' GW think so: Psalm 8:5-8 "constitute a word-by-word commentary and meditation on Genesis 1:26-28."[185]

Yet, it is not possible that David is giving a word-by-word commentary on Genesis 1:26-28; there is no straight line of continuity. The Psalmist's "son of man" cannot be Adam redux because he is the "*son* of man" and not Adam himself. Clearly, we cannot have Adam being the son of *adam*. Nor is this son of man a mere man, as if "son of man", due to parallelism, means only "man" or mankind. Why not? This "man" is at war with his enemies (v2), so David cannot have in mind mankind as a whole when he says "man." Moreover, because it is David writing, one assumes that David is referring to an ideal figure who is also a 'true Israelite', a Davidic son who will reign over the world.[186] Thus, it is prophetic typology that

---

[184] August, "The Messianic Hope of Genesis," 62.

[185] Gentry and Wellum, *Kingdom Through Covenant*, 184, 196. For the same view, see, Martin Pickup, "New Testament Interpretation of the Old Testament: The Theological Rationale of Midrashic Exegesis," *JETS* 51:2 (June, 2008): 363.

[186] Douglas J. Green, "Psalm 8: What is Israel's King That You Remember Him?", *Westminster Theological Seminary* (n.d.), https://students.wts.edu/resources/articles/green.html, accessed 6/12/2018.

is at work in Psalm 8:5-7 and not an exegetical commentary on Genesis 1. "*Son* of man" indicates a figure other than Adam, yet who stems, humanly speaking, from Adam. So, already we are on alert, for we are not dealing with a straight commentary on Genesis 1. It is this "son of man" who was made a little lower than the angels and who rules over the creatures (Psa.8:5). Yet, unless we wish to ignore the Fall, the Noahic Flood, and Genesis 9:4-7, "man" described in Psalm 8 is not a throwback to the prelapsarian order of Adam; rather, the prelapsarian order of Adam is being prophetically projected into the future; for there will be a "son of man" who will prophetically fulfill the dimensions set out by the 'Adamic' imagery. As in the case of the historical Adam, the new, prophetic son of man represents a new humanity, a new Israel; thus, the one represents the many.

Thomas Goodwin puts the Psalm in its proper prophetical setting:

> ...Now I would have you consider likewise the scope of the 8th Psalm, as the apostle brings it....
>
> Now, whereas it is said in the psalm that all things were under his feet, it is not meant of man in innocency, but of the Messiah, Christ and his world, which is made of purpose for him, and the other world was for Adam. That it was not meant of man in innocency properly and prinicipally, appears,
>
> First, because it is said, 'Out of the mouths of babes and sucklings have you ordained strength.' There was no babes and sucklings in Adam's time; he fell before there was any.

Secondly, it is said, 'was to still [*sic*] the enemy and avenger.' But the devil was not stilled by Adam, he overcame him; therefore it must be meant of another that should still this enemy: 'How excellent' says the psalmist, 'is thy name in all the earth,' speaking of this world. Adam he had a paradise, but he never propagated God's name in all the earth, much less did he sound it in the heavens.

Again, Adam, though man, yet he was not the son of man, but called the son of God, he came not of a man.

Again, take the argument the apostle useth; says he, this must have all subject to him, all but God; he must have angels subject to him, for 'he has put all things in subjection under his feet.' This could not be Adam, no, not in the state of innocency; but it is true of Jesus Christ, angels and all were under his feet.

2. As it is not meant of man in innocency, so it cannot be mean of man fallen neither; that is as plain as the other. The apostle himself says, that 'we see not all things subject to him.' Some think that is an objection the apostle answers, but indeed it is a proof to prove that man fallen cannot be meant, for we do not see all things subject to him....[187]

---

[187] Thomas Goodwin, *The Works of Thomas Goodwin, vol. 12* (Edinburgh, UK: James Nichol, 1866), 88-89. See John Williamson Nevin, Philip Schaff, Daniel Gans, *The Incarnate Word: Selected Writings on Christology*, The Mercersburg Theology Study Series, vol.4, ser. ed. William B. Evans, (Eugene, OR: Wipf Stock, 2014), 193-194.

Thus, Psalm 8:5-7 is not a commentary of man in his state of innocence,[188] but of Man in the new world, a world in which God's enemies are defeated and where praise comes from the mouth of babes. This is the world of the promise, a world where the Serpent and his evil seed have been destroyed, and the Seed, the true Man, has succeeded. From a canonical perspective, as Goodwin wrote, we know the son of man as the Son of Man, the Last Man, Jesus Christ.

What we should also understand about Psalm 8 is that it depicts the Davidic son.[189] This is David's promised seed (*zera*) (2 Sam.7:12). Again, the seed is an individual who represents many. Picking up on the imagery of Genesis 3:15, the Davidic son will wound (*machats*) the head (leader) (*rosh*) of many lands he is at war with (Psa.110:6; see Psa.3:7; 68:22). Likewise, in Psalm 72, the

---

[188] *Contra* Brandon D. Crowe, *The Last Adam: A Theology of the Obedient Life of Jesus in the Gospels* (Grand Rapids, MI: Baker Academic, 2017), 23-54.

[189] Yahweh had drilled David to understand that the world hated God and his Anointed, and that Yahweh God will subdue his enemies, which were the enemies of David and his people, Israel (e.g., 2 Sam.7; Psa.2; 110; etc.). Some scholars reject the interpretation that the Davidic son and the son of man are the same individual, on the basis that the Davidic son was not a ruler over *the nations*. I beg to differ. In Psalms 2 and 110, it is apparent that the LORD has set apart an individual who is royal, who is distinct to Israel, to deliver Israel. The deliverer is a "king," "anointed," a "son" who is "begotten" (Psa.2). This deliverer is a "lord", a "priest after the order of Melchizedek", who has a scepter and sits at God's right hand (Psa.110). Patently, this person is the Davidic son, God's 'son.' The Davidic son's eternal reign is taught in Psalm 18; 132; Isaiah 9:1-7; 16:1-5; 55; Jeremiah 23:1-8; 30:1-17; 33; Ezekiel 34; and Hosea 3:5. These verses refer to the Davidic king ruling in Israel over his enemies. The Davidic king's majesty is evident to the whole earth: Psalm 89:27 refers to the Davidic son as the most exalted king of the earth; also, Jeremiah 33:9 refers to Jerusalem, as led by David's son, which is blessed so fully by God that the nations of the world see it and rejoice.

Davidic king will overpower his enemies and have dominion over them (v2; see Gen.1:26-28). And in Psalm 72:9, the Davidic son's enemies are described as bowing before him and licking the dust, "Let the nomads of the desert bow before him, And his enemies lick the dust."[190] Thus, in Psalm 8, prelapsarian Adam is not the prototype of salvation. Rather, the prelapsarian order is utilized in a prophetic manner to magnify a son of man, the Davidic son, the seed of David, who will fulfill the promise of the Seed of the woman.

Daniel's Son of Man

More of this "son of man" is spoken of in Daniel 7:13. To GW's credit, they do describe the Danielic "son of man" as a divine figure who represents Israel.[191] Daniel 7 is fulfilled in Jesus Christ, the heavenly Man.[192] Although G. K. Beale also works with a line of continuity between Adam and Christ, I agree when he writes:

> ...Jesus is a Last Adam figure, and this is partly why he implicitly identifies himself with Daniel's 'Son of Man' in issuing the universal commission to his followers: he is the 'son of Adam', the equivalent to Daniel's 'Son of Man', finally accomplishing...what Daniel predicts the messianic end-time Adam would do.[193]

---

[190] Chou, *Hermeneutics of Biblical Writers*, 88.

[191] Gentry and Wellum, *Kingdom Through Covenant*, 531, 542, 560, 562.

[192] G. K. Beale, *The Book of Revelation*, NIGTC, (Grand Rapids, MI: William B. Eerdmans Publishing Company, 1999), 221-222.

[193] G. K. Beale, *The Temple and the Church's Mission: A Biblical Theology of the Dwelling Place of God*, NSBT, ser. ed., D. A. Carson, (Downers Grove, Ill: IVP Academic, 2004), 169. For an extensive discussion of the "son of man" as the Last Adam, see Yongbom Lee,

Likewise, although I do not accept the critical presuppositions of Peter B. Ely, he is correct to comment:

> ...though the figure of the Son of Man leads us back to the initial figure, it is not identical with the Adam of Genesis: The Son of Man is Man; but he is no longer the First Man, but a Man who is coming; he is the Man of the end, whether he be an individual or the personification of a collective entity, of the remnant of Israel, or of the whole of humanity" (Ricoeur 1967, 268). The figure of the Son of Man looks toward the future, to a kingdom that is to come, something we have not yet seen, rather than to the simple restoration of a state of being that was lost. In this sense, the figure of the Son of Man shares something of the "grace abounding" so prominent in Paul's designation of Christ as the Second Adam.[194]

Some scholars state that the Danielic son of man corresponds to the Seed of the woman. The son of man will defeat cosmic powers, crushing the head of the Serpent, that is, the son of man destroys the beasts, who, too, embody Satan's power (see Rev.13:1-2; John 12:31; 14:30; Luke 4:5-6).[195]

The Son of Man as the Last Adam: The Early Church Tradition as a Source of Paul's Adam Christology (Eugene, OR: Pickwick Publications, 2012).

[194] Peter B. Ely, *Adam and Eve in Scripture, Theology, and Literature: Sin, Compassion, and Forgiveness* (Lanham, MD: Lexington Books, 2018), 97.

[195] Robert Jamieson, *et. al.*, *A Commentary, Critical and Explanatory, on the Old and New Testaments, Volumes 1-2* (Hartford, CT: S. S. Scranton & Company, 1872), 635; Benjamin Kennicott, *A Sermon*

CONCLUSION

I demonstrated in the exegetical section that there is no such thing as an AC. To be pointed, there was no need for an Adamic *covenant* because there was no division in human society and no division between God and man. Sin, death, Satan, and the curse were not forces needing to be subdued. It was only after man almost exterminated himself through the Flood that God instituted the covenant for the first time, in order to preserve foolish man and to bring to pass the promise of the Seed. None of this was done in 'fulfillment' of an AC.

Yet, because the paradigm of interpretation used by GW relies heavily on a BT model that strongly resembles CT and its teaching about the continuity of the covenants, they were compelled to defend an AC. The difference was that GW began with the AC and drew a straight line of continuity from it to the NC. It was only when they entered into NT territory that GW started to exhibit NCT principles. In other words, GW's Progressive Covenantalisim system owed more to CT than it did to NCT.

Preached Before the University of Oxford at St. Mary's Church (Oxford, England: Theatre, 1765), 50-51; Karl August Auberlen, Magnus Friedrich Roos, *The Prophecies of Daniel and the Revelations of St. John, Viewed in Their Mutual Relation, With an Exposition of the Principle Passages*, transl. Adolph Saphir, (New York: Wiley and Halsted, 1857), 42; N.A., *On the Numbers in Daniel* (Madras, India: Church Mission Press, 1836), 7. See Delbert Burkett, *The Son of Man Debate: A History and Evaluation*, Society for New Testament Studies, Monography Series 107, (Cambridge, UK: Cambridge University Press, 2004), 9-10; Hebert Lockyer, *All the Messianic Prophecies of the Bible* (Grand Rapids, MI: Zondervan, 1988), 112.

The unique nature of GW's line of continuity thesis was that the AC was the hermeneutical foundation of all the other divine covenants. As such, it obviated the centrality of the *protoevangelium*, making it a mere building block in a grammatically-historically correct and wooden reading of the biblical text that smothered any negative assessment of the Adamic administration or of Adam himself. Canonically, the negative canonical assessment that the NT placed upon Adam was not connected, by GW, with the OT's record of Adam and the use of 'Adamic' imagery.

In contrast to GW, in placing the *protogevangelium* at the forefront of interpretation, it entailed that covenants support the evangelical promise of the Seed, and not the other way round. In that setting, the OT utilized the failed Adamic administration, seconding it and its 'Adamic' imagery in service of the fulfillment of the promise of the Seed. It is for that reason alone, Genesis 9 and Psalm 8, for example, employ 'Adamic' themes, as they lay down yet another layer of prophetic anticipation.

Moreover, a proper reading of the Adamic administration showed, as 1 Corinthians 15 demonstrated, that Adam's relationship with God was built upon earthly principles and not heavenly. Even if Adam had not sinned, his subsequent state would never have been heavenly or immortal. Christ alone is the heavenly Man. That is why, ultimately, the NC and a so-called AC, cannot be compared, nor can one draw a positive line of continuity from one to the other.